Anthony —
Best wishes and have
a great birthday!
Rob
x x

Anthony —
Have a lovely
Birthday month
happy returns
holly x

Since you were born,
you have enjoyed 50
birthdays, and Wolves have
beaten Burnley 30 times
(compared to Burnley's 13
wins). Long may your birthdays + Wolves wins continue.
To a great boss + a top man
all round.
James

Have a fantastic
birthday — hope
you like the
surprise!
Love Georgina
X

# The Twentieth Century's
# Greatest Cart

GW00587233

Sponsored by the Political Cartoon Society
and BBC History Magazine

Hope you have
a great birthday
Anthony and. N
also hope Burnley
manage to recieve
more points this
year than you've
had years!
Best Wishes
Neil

Anthony —
Happy 50th! Have
a great evening! and
happy reading!
love Beccy x

Dear Anthony 50th
A very Happy Enjoy
Birthday. Enjoy
the book
Best Wishes
Rachael x

Hope that these
cartoons stir up a few-
but not too many-
memories from the
past 50 years.

fondest wishes
Jude
X

3

Low! The Twentieth Century's Greatest Cartoonist

Published by BBC History Magazine,
BBC Worldwide Ltd, Woodlands,
80 Wood Lane, London W12 0TT

First published 2002

ISBN: 0563 488557

Set in Garamond and Helvetica Neue by Garden House Press
Printed and bound in Great Britain by Garden House Press

# Contents

THE RECRUITING PARADE.

ALL BEHIND YOU, WINSTON

"ME, TOO!"

# Foreword

*by Tony Banks, MP for West Ham*

IT IS THE ability to get under the skin of the powerful and show us the political reality behind their words and deeds that is the mark of the truly great cartoonist. In this respect, Sir David Low is probably Britain's greatest cartoonist of the 20th century, and an exemplar of the genre.

Low's caricatures of politicians are dramatic, and incisive. His cartoons of the 1930s exposed the true evils of Fascism and Nazism at a time when many politicians, in Britain and elsewhere, were either ignorant of their menace or – worse – naive or craven apologists. Nor was Low content to toe any party political line, nor that of his proprietor. It was this that gave his work its continuing vigour.

There are still some who believe that the cartoonist is neither a true artist nor a significant political commentator. On both counts they are wrong. From Hogarth to Peter Brookes, the work of the cartoonist has impacted upon the artistic and political scene.

That is why, as chairman of the House of Commons Advisory Committee on Works of Art, I wish to express my gratitude to Mr Speaker and the Lord Chancellor for their permission to hold the exhibition, *Low! The Twentieth Century's Greatest Cartoonist*, in Westminster Hall. We are also grateful to *BBC History Magazine* for sponsoring the exhibition, and to Dr Tim Benson, whose original idea it was, and who has done so much to bring it into being.

My committee is also charged with acquiring and commissioning works of art which mark political events and personalities. All art forms are represented in the collection, and the Works of Art Committee has contributed a number of original Low cartoons to the exhibition from a collection presented to the House by David Low himself.

My committee hopes to continue using this historic heart of the Palace of Westminster for exhibitions and events which commemorate and celebrate the development of Parliamentary democracy in our country. Exhibitions to mark the impeachment of Warren Hastings, and the relationship between Parliament and the American War of Independence are currently in the planning stage. Meanwhile, I am sure that this exhibition of the works of David Low will give as much enjoyment – and food for thought – to all those who see it.

# David Low as a cartoonist

*by Alan Mumford, author of 'Stabbed in the Front: Post-War General Elections through Political Cartoons'*

DAVID LOW'S reputation as one of the 20th century's greatest cartoonists rests on the unforgettable images he created in the 1930s and '40s. Perhaps these cartoons have been given undue prominence because of the significant events that inspired them; as this exhibition shows, they were not necessarily his most effective works. Low's cartoons were perceived as powerful long before Hitler's government protested about them in 1937.

## Low's life

David Alexander Cecil Low was born on 7 April 1891 in Dunedin, New Zealand. His first published cartoon appeared when he was 11, and after leaving school he worked as a political cartoonist in New Zealand. By 1911, Low had moved to Australia and was drawing cartoons for the *Sydney Bulletin*. In 1919, he left Australia to join one of London's three evening papers, the *Star*. This exhibition starts, in effect, when Low moved to the *Evening Standard* in 1927. In 1950, Low left the *Standard* for the *Daily Herald*, and in 1953, he moved to the *Manchester Guardian*. Low was knighted in 1962 and died in September 1963.

## The *Evening Standard*

Major influences on Low at the *Standard* included Lord Beaverbrook, the paper's proprietor. Beaverbrook had pursued Low for years, despite the fact that his cartoons often opposed Beaverbrook's policies. Beaverbrook was described as impish in his relations with political friends (and malicious to his enemies); he enjoyed stirring up trouble. And when Low caused trouble,

**David Low: the master at his drawing board**

Beaverbrook claimed that Low's contractual freedom meant he had no control over him.

While the *Evening Standard* competed with the *Star* and the *Evening News* for readers, it was the favourite evening paper of the wealthier classes in London and the south east of England. It was, therefore, more widely read than its rivals by people of influence, particularly MPs. But, despite its influence, it was a London, not a national, paper. Low's cartoons would possibly have had even more impact if they had appeared in one of the national broadsheets. Some of these had

cartoonists: the *Daily Express*, the *Daily Herald* and the *Daily Mail*, for example. But the heavy broadsheets – *The Times*, *The Daily Telegraph* and the then *Manchester Guardian* – did not.

## Intention and influence

Low had strong views about the best style in which to present his ideas. He distinguished his political satire from purely humorous cartoons. He wrote that 'no artist in caricature purely can do good work on malice. It clouds the judgement. The immoderate exaggeration inspired by malice is apt to become as tedious as too much slapstick in a farce… Brutality almost invariably defeats itself'. In 1935, he was already attacking Nazi Germany. And when the war came he expressed a similar view: 'The horrific cartoon is not an effective political approach in this war. What the dictator does not want to get around is the idea that he is an ass, which is really damaging.'

Low said he attacked policies rather than personalities. He did not distort faces or bodies; he was generous to Lloyd George, for example, portraying him as a happy imp, although Low disapproved of him. The offence taken by some of his targets surprised him. Although Low's anti-appeasement, anti-Nazi cartoons have arguably been given an unbalanced prominence, others believed that they were very influential indeed. Michael Foot, who worked with Low as acting editor on the *Evening Standard*, said 'Low contributed more than any other single figure, and changed the way people saw Hitler.' If this seems exaggerated, the Nazis certainly thought his work worth attention in the 1930s. A Low cartoon in November 1933 commented on the burning of the German Reichstag, and the subsequent elimination of the Nazis' enemies. Immediately, the *Standard* was banned in Germany, and Beaverbrook was told that it would remain forbidden as long as Low was its cartoonist. Since the cartoons were not published in Germany, it is clear that the Nazis were worried about their influence in Britain and around the world. Low was certainly leaned on by the then Foreign Secretary, Lord Halifax, to tone down his criticisms, and he did make some adjustments. Low later said Halifax had told him that Hitler had his cartoons spread in front of him once a week.

In Britain, Low cartoons attracted both support and criticism. Winston Churchill said of his 1924 cartoon 'The Recruiting Parade' (cartoon 3): 'there is not a figure in it that is not instinct with maliciously perceived truth'; he was surprised when Lord Birkenhead took profound offence at it. Churchill said that Low was a 'green-eyed, young, Antipodean radical, a master of black and white; he is the Charlie Chaplin of caricature'. He added that Low was 'the greatest of our modern caricaturists, deriding regularly everything that is of importance to our self-preservation'. As wartime Prime Minister, however, Churchill could be censorious, attempting to stop the film based on Low's Colonel Blimp.

Low's contract with the *Standard* gave him the same freedom that he had enjoyed on the *Star*. 'It is agreed that you are to have complete freedom in the selection and treatment of subject matter for your cartoons and in the expression therein of the policies in which you believe.' The contract, though, did not mean that the *Standard* had to print *anything* Low drew, and some cartoons were not published. But it suited both Beaverbrook and Low to emphasise his independence, and say nothing if his cartoons did not appear ('Hard Lot of a Cartoonist', 13 October 1927, cartoon 6).

Tim Benson has suggested that part of Beaverbrook's contented relationship with Low may have related to Low's frequent inclusion of Beaverbrook in his cartoons, to a greater extent than the Press lord's real political strength justified. Low himself confessed that he frequently drew Beaverbrook smiling, though Beaverbrook smiled

**Gad, sir, Citrine is right. The Labour Party is quite right to expel all but sound Conservatives.**

**BLIMP'S PURGE**

**Low with his creation, the ultra-reactionary Col. Blimp**

no more than other men. Certainly the portrayal of Beaverbrook is puckish.

Before the period represented here, Low had produced a devastating critique of the Coalition Government of the early 1920s: a two-headed ass 'without pride of ancestry or hope of posterity'. One head was Lloyd George and those Liberals who clung to him, the other head was the Conservative majority. During the period covered here, perhaps his most distinctive characterisations were those of Lord Birkenhead (a brilliant lawyer who never hid his intelligence) as Lord Burstinghead ('Recruiting Parade', 7 October 1924, cartoon 3), and the Labour Minister Jimmy Thomas, who was satirised as 'Rt Hon Dress Suit', because of his supposed attachment to the costume of a class into which he had not been born. While these were exaggerations of individuals, Low also created the Trade Union Carthorse to represent the solidarity and immobility of the trade union movement. Most famous of all is

Colonel Blimp (left), who appeared for the first time in April 1934. Low emphasised that Blimp represented stupidity of every kind; in this collection we see him as a hotel manager (7 September 1943, cartoon 49) and a workman (12 February 1947, cartoon 60).

Low was the first cartoonist in Britain to put himself in his own work, usually to make a comment extending the ideas in the cartoon. Low's contemporary, Strube, used a 'little man' to the same end. Low's eminence was given establishment recognition when he was knighted. Other cartoonists had been similarly honoured before him – Tenniel, Leslie Ward ('Spy'), Francis Carruthers Gould, Bernard Partridge. Low, however, was (so far) the last of the line.

This exhibition demonstrates that Low's body of work can truly be defined by the American title of one of his books: *History of our Times*.

## THE HISTORICAL CONTEXT

Historical ocurrences are sometimes described as being like comets, with an extraordinary event flashing across the political sky, leaving a visible trail. Therefore, although the first cartoon in the exhibition is from 1924, understanding it depends on a knowledge of earlier events, which are summarised here.

Low's representations of political events until 1929 centred primarily on the Liberal Party, and the First World War. The Liberals, who had been in power since 1906, were led by Herbert Asquith into the Great War in 1914. In 1915, he formed a coalition government embracing the Conservative Party. In 1916, Asquith was replaced as Prime Minister by his most vigorous party colleague, David Lloyd George. But Lloyd George carried with him only part of the Liberal Party – others remained loyal to Asquith or distrustful of Lloyd George.

In 1918, with the war over, Lloyd George called a general election known as the 'coupon election'. This referred to the fact that Lloyd George and his Conservative coalition partner Bonar Law gave their personal 'coupon' of support to candidates in their parties who supported the Lloyd George government. This deepened the split in the Liberal

Party, creating antagonistic Asquithian and Lloyd George factions. Lloyd George survived in office until 1922 with the support of the Conservatives, by then the largest party in the Commons. But in 1922, Conservative MPs, at a meeting in the Carlton Club, withdrew their support. The Conservatives won the subsequent election. Lloyd George remained a force in British politics for another ten years, but never got near to power again. Bonar Law, described by his biographer Lord Blake as 'The Unknown Prime Minister', took over.

Several talented Tories did not immediately make themselves available for office, including Austen Chamberlain, who had been party leader until the revolt against Lloyd George. He epitomised Churchill's description of him: 'he always played the game – and always lost it'. In his absence, Stanley Baldwin succeeded the unknown Prime Minister as the unknown Chancellor of the Exchequer, and eventually became Prime Minister himself – only to lose an unnecessary election in 1924.

In that election, Labour became the second largest party. Baldwin thought it a good idea that they should acquire an understanding of the realities of politics by forming a minority government. This lasted only nine months, and in an election at the end of 1924, the Conservatives were returned. With them came Winston Churchill, elected as a Constitutionalist, and awarded the job of Chancellor of the Exchequer. Churchill had left the Liberal Party to become an anti-socialist candidate (see 'Recruiting Parade', 7 October 1924, cartoon 3).

## The 1920s and 1930s

As a result of the emergence of Labour and the fissures in the Liberals, politics remained fluid through the 1920s. Labour was led by Ramsay MacDonald, the first genuinely working-class British Prime Minister. Self-educated, he held audiences spellbound with aspirational but empty oratory; Churchill characterised him as 'the boneless wonder'. Several senior Conservatives who had held aloof from Baldwin's first Government joined his second – notably

Top Tories: (l to r) Lord Birkenhead, Neville Chamberlain and Walter Guinness during the May 1926 General Strike

Austen Chamberlain, as Foreign Secretary, and Lord Birkenhead. This Government lasted its full five-year term but rising unemployment brought defeat in 1929. For the first time, Labour was the largest party in the Commons, though still without an overall majority. The Liberals, uneasily reunited under Lloyd George, had attempted to recover with the slogan 'We can conquer unemployment'.

Labour's lack of a majority made for difficult government, and the party had no real idea how to convert socialist principles into effective legislation. Unemployment grew alarmingly. The Government was unable to agree on what to do, and eventually broke up over cutting social benefits. The problems of the British economy were exacerbated by the 1929 Wall Street Crash.

In 1931, MacDonald, in what was seen by most of his party as a great betrayal, resigned as Labour Prime Minister only to reappear as Prime Minister of a National Government with a few of his Labour colleagues, some Conservatives, and a sprinkling of Liberals. Neville Chamberlain, Austen's half-brother, became Chancellor. MacDonald remained the decayed figurehead of a government described as National but now almost wholly Conservative until 1935. Baldwin again became the actual as well as the *de facto* Prime Minister in 1935, and won the subsequent General Election – still as a National Prime Minister. He was faced with continuing high unemployment, to which the government had no solutions, as well as other major issues: the unique constitutional crisis caused by the abdication of Edward VIII, and Hitler's resurgent Germany.

## Churchill and India

Before he became Prime Minister, Baldwin had pushed through a bill giving a very modest element of involvement in the government of their country to the people of India. Churchill violently opposed the proposals and left the Conservative Front Bench. He described Gandhi, the pacific leader of the Indian independence movement, as 'a half naked Fakir'. Such opinions kept Churchill out of the 1931 National Government ('Between Gandhi and Windhi', 31 January 1931, cartoon 11).

## The Abdication

India was one of three major issues on which Churchill was out of line with his Conservative party colleagues. The abdication of Edward VIII, in which he supported the errant King, was the second. Churchill's involvement on Edward's side increased the suspicion in which Churchill was held, and meant that his more substantial criticisms of the government over German rearmament did not gain proper attention. Edward had succeeded to the throne in 1936; his affair with Wallis Warfield Simpson, a twice-divorced American, was in full flow. But British newspaper publishers agreed to

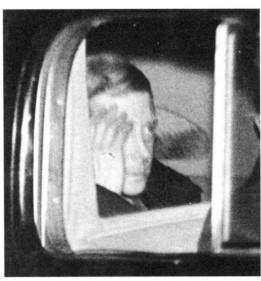

**King over the water: Edward VIII drives into French exile after abdicating in December 1936 to marry Mrs Simpson**

conceal the liasion from their readers. Prime Minister Baldwin made it clear to Edward that his intention to marry Mrs Simpson was unacceptable if he wished to remain King. Edward eventually abdicated to marry Mrs Simpson; the cartoons of 9 and 11 December 1936 here (18 and 19) do not comment directly on either party.

## Labour in opposition after 1931

After Labour's annihilation at the hands of the National Government in the 1931 election, George Lansbury was elected as Leader of the surviving 46 Labour MPs. Lansbury's pacifism led to his destruction by Ernest Bevin at the Party Conference in 1935, immediately before the General Election ('Another ascent into the strato-sphere', 11 September 1935, cartoon 13). Clement Attlee, his deputy, succeeded him. Labour's position on foreign affairs was a belief in collective security through the League of Nations. However, they voted against defence budgets and conscription. Labour did not trust the National Government – but its negative votes on these issues made its anti-appeasement claims unconvincing.

## Appeasement and the Dictators

The Great War had ended in November 1918 with a determination from the victorious Allies that it should be 'the war to end wars', and that Germany should be made to pay reparations for the damage it had caused. But the attempt to wring payments out of Germany was one reason that the former objective failed.

The rise of Hitler's Nazis was built on a number of causes, notably the desire to recover lost German territory and national self-respect. Hitler's arrival in power in 1933 led to illegal rearmament and the re-occupation of the German Rhineland in 1936. The Western powers did nothing about this, either; many thought it reasonable that Germany should reoccupy its own 'backyard'.

Baldwin was unwilling to confront voters in the 1935 General Election with the need for British re-armament: 'my lips are sealed'. Undoubtedly, he would have been swimming against the tide of a pacific public opinion if he had been more honest about what needed to be done.

Baldwin's successor as Prime Minister in 1937, Neville Chamberlain, was more explicit. He set about a modest programme of rearmament, but at the same time hoped his appeasement policy would avoid conflict with Hitler. Appeasement accepted Germany's claims but hoped that territorial change could be peaceful. In practice, this meant that as Hitler pursued his aims, Chamberlain and his Cabinet colleagues found reasons for allowing him to achieve them. Hitler's claim to embrace the Germans in the Sudetenland in Czechoslovakia was accepted by France and Britain in October 1938, who bullied the Czechs into accepting it too.

Churchill's was a lone voice predicting disaster. In contrast, Chamberlain talked about the threat to Czechoslovakia as 'a quarrel in a far away county between people of whom we know nothing'. (Increasing Pressure, 18 February 1938, cartoon 34). Chamberlain went to Munich, returning with 'a piece of paper signed by Herr Hitler'; Hitler took the rump of Czechoslovakia in March 1939. Austria too fell into Germany's arms. Britain and

**Neville Chamberlain returns from Munich after meeting Hitler and Mussolini (right) in October 1938**

France were finally faced with trying to stop Hitler invading Poland, without the means to do so. Soviet Russia, faced with what it saw as the weakness of Britain and France, made its own agreement with Germany to share the dismemberment of Poland and take over the Baltic States.

Hitler believed that the German people were of pure Aryan stock ('I demand that German blood be pure', 5 December 1935, cartoon 27). When this was joined by his conviction that Jews were responsible for many of Germany's problems, it led to the barbarism of the concentration camps in which Jews and other despised people were exterminated.

In Italy, Mussolini, the fascist leader, attempted to recreate the glories of the Roman Empire, in particular by a war on what was then called Abyssinia, now Ethiopia ('Barbarism/Civilization', 11 October 1935, cartoon 25). Both Hitler and Mussolini were also involved in a third European dictatorship, that of Franco in Spain who had through civil war overturned the legitimate government ('You've got to admit...', 21 June 1937, cartoon 31). Here again Britain and France stood to one side, operating a policy of 'non-intervention'. Germany and Italy, in contrast, cheerfully used the Spanish Civil War to test their planes, pilots and troops.

In Asia, Japan, too, was expansionist. In fact, they were the first aggressors to show that the League of Nations was incapable of taking effective physical action to preserve peace when they attacked China, first Manchuria (1931), then Shanghai (1932).

## The Second World War

Chamberlain's guarantee of Poland's borders was unsuccessful; Hitler was prepared to go to war if necessary. Russia and Germany's non-aggression pact surprised those who thought their conflicting ideologies would be more important than their perceptions of immediate national interest ('Someone is taking someone for a walk', 2 November 1939, cartoon 40).

Chamberlain, who had resisted taking the belligerent Churchill into his government, put him in charge of the Admiralty once the Second World War started. But Chamberlain was not an effective war leader. A disastrous expedition to save Norway from German invasion led to Lloyd George's last significant parliamentary speech, and loss of support forced Chamberlain to resign. The Labour Party, which had refused to join Chamberlain in a National Government, now agreed to serve under Churchill ('All behind you, Winston', 14 May 1940, cartoon 42).

Churchill faced disaster beyond anything Asquith and Lloyd George had experienced in the First World War, as the Germans overran Belgium, Holland and France. The extraordinary evacuation from Dunkirk in June 1940 emphasised the fact that Britain was left with no European allies. Only the continued support of the Commonwealth, and Churchill's intention to try and seduce the United States into the war, held out hope for the future ('Very Well, Alone', 18 June 1940, cartoon 44).

Italy had entered the war late against France and Britain but showed itself less capable of defeating Greece than it was of bombing the undefended people of Abyssinia ('A sad tale of a punctured chin', 25 November 1940, cartoon 46). However, Germany came to Mussolini's aid, and defeats continued for the Allies in Greece, Crete and North Africa. At home, the *Luftwaffe* attempted to batter Britain into submission by bombing civilians, a practice begun by the Germans but finished by the Allied air forces at the end of the war ('Impregnable Target', 11 September 1940, cartoon 45).

Hitler, having shared Poland with Soviet Russia, invaded Russia in June 1941 – a decision that, with America's entry into the war in December 1941, eventually sealed his fate. Churchill's assertion that

People's party: Clement Attlee (centre) waves to well-wishers after Labour's election landslide win in July 1945

Britain had used up its foreign reserves to fight the war and was dependent on American aid to survive. President Harry Truman's Secretary of State, George Marshall, produced the 'Marshall Plan', which provided financial support for many European countries.

## Return of the Conservatives

Mild-mannered, low-key Attlee had triumphed over the wild election claims by Churchill that Britain would have a 'Gestapo' if Labour won. Churchill may or may not have described his wartime deputy as a 'modest little man with plenty to be modest about'. By 1951, however, the Labour Government was exhausted, the economic problems following the war were blamed on it, and Churchill at 77 became a peacetime Tory Prime Minister for the first time.

He returned to office with stronger views about foreign policy (particularly about the need to reach an agreement to prevent nuclear war) than he did about domestic policy. There was no big effort to reverse Labour legislation – the nationalised industries remained nationalised.

Churchill suffered two strokes in office, but managed to conceal the fact. His 80th birthday celebration (November 1954) gave him the opportunity for a final flourish: he and his wife hated the official portrait by Graham Sutherland presented to him by Parliament so much that it was later destroyed; he much preferred the painting given to him by Low (number 71).

Stalin died in 1953. He was succeeded by Khrushchev, who made a secret speech in 1956 in which he criticised the evils of Stalinism from which he had himself, of course, benefited ('Early Spring Clean', 20 March 1956, cartoon 72). Khrushchev was, however, unwilling to relax the Soviet grip on the Eastern European countries 'freed' during the war than Stalin had been. The first significant attempt to loosen it, made in 1956 by a reforming communist government in Hungary, led to its bloody suppression by Russian soldiers and tanks ('People's democracy', 16 November 1956, cartoon 75).

he would co-operate with the devil if Hitler invaded Hell may have been surprising because of his previous attacks on Bolshevism, but not in terms of the exigencies of war ('Battle for Britain – Part 2', 25 July 1941, cartoon 47).

## Labour in power

Labour declined to continue in a National Government with Churchill once the war against Germany had been won. Churchill reverted from admired war leader to his pre-war guise of bitter belligerence against his opponents. People packed the streets to cheer him as he toured the country during the election, but many voted against him.

In July 1945, Labour was returned to power with a landslide majority for the first time. The distinction between the Churchill personas was caught brilliantly by Low in 'Two Churchills', 31 July 1945 (cartoon 56). Clement Attlee, the accidental Labour Leader in 1935, led a Labour government with a reforming agenda much clearer than its minority predecessors had ever had. While its domestic agenda (the nationalisation of major industries, the creation of the National Health Service) was totally different from that of the Conservatives, foreign policy under Ernest Bevin was not a matter of huge difference between the parties; there were more schisms within the Labour Party about appropriate attitudes to Soviet Russia and the United States ('Continuity of foreign policy', 30 July 1945, cartoon 55).

The Soviet invasion of Hungary coincided with the British and French attempt, in collusion with Israel, to take control of the Suez Canal in 1956. Justified as an attempt to free the canal from the grasp of the Egyptian dictator, Colonel Nasser, it led to the canal being blocked for months, and to a humiliating Anglo-French withdrawal under US pressure. This action was led by Anthony Eden, who had taken over from Churchill in 1955. Suez saw Eden attempting action that he had not encouraged in relation to Germany in 1936 ('Me Too', 6 November 1956, cartoon 74). Broken in health, Eden resigned in 1957.

The indignities of racial prejudice were highlighted on two different continents. In the US, discrimination against blacks finally led to a series of civic revolts ('Alabama', 28 February 1956, cartoon 73). Harold Macmillan, who had replaced Eden as Prime Minister, went to apartheid South Africa to talk about 'a wind of change' sweeping through the continent. His thrust was not only that Britain was releasing colonies into independence, but that such change was inevitable ('In the name of Africa...', 5 January 1960, cartoon 77). The South African response was to make apartheid even more rigid and demeaning to its non-white population.

Britain's relationship with the rest of the world after 1945 was dominated by the issue of nuclear weapons, and later by how far Britain should be part of a new Europe. The war in Japan had ended in August 1945 when America dropped atomic bombs on Hiroshima and Nagasaki; their devastating effect was rapidly revealed to the world. Discussion of the morality of using atomic weapons became more pointed as relations between Russia and the West deteriorated after the war and Russia acquired nuclear weapons, partly thanks to its spies in the west.

Although Attlee's government had developed atomic weapons, the Labour Party was split on the issue; for many the prospect of ending the world by nuclear warfare was completely unacceptable. The Campaign for Nuclear Disarmament (CND) wanted Britain to disarm unilaterally. However,

Hugh Gaitskell, Leader of the Labour Party after Attlee from 1955, wished to retain the potential to use nuclear weapons ('History repeats itself', 29 April 1960, cartoon 79).

Labour was split, too, on the issue of the extent to which Britain should be part of the European Economic Community (now the EU). Macmillan's Conservative Government fruitlessly pursued entry, although Churchill had declined to participate at its formation ('Camel and the eye of the needle', 13 October 1961, cartoon 82).

## CARTOONISTS ON LOW

### Ronald Searle

*Best known for his illustrations of St Trinian's School, and Nigel Molesworth*

❛ Low was indisputably one of the most vigorous, independent and outspoken political caricaturists since the middle of the 19th century. The limitations demanded in drawing for mass circulation newspapers are both technical and moral. Low, in so far as his jealously guarded independence and concern for integrity would allow him, successfully came to terms with topicality, newsprint, and what he referred to as 'the level demanded by the perceptivity of the bonehead' – the reader.

Throughout his long and demanding career, Low's drawing retained an incredible sureness of touch. There was something of an oriental facility in his handling of the brush. But underneath those broad and self-assured strokes was a careful and conscientious construction in pencil.

The political cartoonist can only thrive in opposition. Low was particularly fortunate in not only enjoying for most of his life opposition in politics, but also for a number of years being employed by a proprietor who encouraged his opposition to the paper that printed his drawings. Given this fortunate set of circumstances – the *Evening Standard*, Lord Beaverbrook, Hitler and Mussolini – Low produced his best work. He was able to respond

to his times with the same kind of melodramatic simplicity as did Gillray; the issues were black and white. Given the additional advantage of his own positive views and a cast of flamboyant personalities, he was able to fuse his idealism, his cynicism, and his talent into a whole and produce some of the most outstanding and powerful political cartoons since Gillray fathered the art. ❜

### Steve Bell

*Cartoonist for The Guardian*

❛ David Low set the standard for political cartooning in British newspapers a very long time ago and that standard has held, more or less unchallenged, ever since. His style was so distinct, so clear, and so modern that it's difficult to imagine now what papers were like before he got into his stride in the 1920s. Two things define him: his inimitable brushwork and his forthright opinions about contemporary politics. The former is quite simply dazzling: when you look at a Low original it almost vibrates with a kind of Op Art vitality, and that's without mentioning his skill at caricature. His line was very thick, but very intelligent.

As to his opinions: firstly and most importantly he had some. He was a leftie operating in primarily right-wing papers. It's no secret he was widely loathed as well as loved, ending up on the Gestapo death list, where of course every right-thinking person should have aspired to be.

A small and very ancient volume, published by Penguin Books in the first years of the war, demonstrates his dominance. It's called *Europe since Versailles* and simply tells the history of the period from 1919 to 1940 using Low's cartoons and absolutely minimal captions of no more than one line. The story is so clear and so well told it absolutely speaks for itself, and it culminates with his best known cartoon: 'Rendezvous', where Hitler and Stalin greet each other over the corpse of Poland. This image is so striking, so pertinent, so accurate and so blindingly obvious that all we can do once we've seen it is take it for granted.

He was on top of his trade for so long that it's hardly surprising that he should occasionally sound a note of pomposity, particularly in his later years when his journalistic hegemony was over and he finally accepted a knighthood. He obviously thought he was God's gift, and for most of the twenties, thirties and forties, for all intents and purposes, he was.'

### Martin Rowson
*Cartoonist; his work has appeared in The Guardian, The Daily Mirror, The Times, The Scotsman, Tribune and The Independent on Sunday*

'If I was ever asked what the most influential book I'd ever read was I'd have to say *An Illustrated History of Modern Britain* by Denis Richards (MA) and JW Hunt (MA), published by Longmans in 1950. I got hold of this volume when I was about eight, and the point about it was that it's illustrated exclusively with contemporary cartoons commenting on the history told. Thus at an early and impressionable age I was introduced to the work of Gillray, Rowlandson, Cruickshank, Tenniel and, most of all, Low. I haven't looked back.

Low was, and still is, a revelation. Although my style developed in a totally opposite direction to Low's simple and fluid line, Low showed me, growing up when Scarfe and Steadman ruled the roost, that you can be just as savage in intent without necessarily being savage in execution, and above all that the most potent satirical tool is not just to horrify your readers but also to make them laugh. As a Tory MP observed during the war, Low's record of making the Nazis look 'bloody fools' was infinitely more effective than all the official anti-Nazi propaganda put together. His position on the Gestapo's Death List is rather grim icing on the cake.

Of course, he also bequeathed later cartoonists a magnificent legacy of enduringly potent political images. Most of us have nicked 'Rendezvous' or the TUC carthorse or 'Very Well, Alone' at some point or other. I think my favourite Low creation – because it was so intrinsically funny – was one of his earliest. The Coalition Ass, a small, sterile, and rather cute pushmepullyou, summed up Lloyd George's post-First World War coalition government perfectly. I tried to revive it as a symbol of the Liberal-SDP Alliance during the 1987 election when I was working on *Today*. My effort at plagiarism was vetoed by the then editor as being too sophisticated for the readers, which probably says more about newspaper editors than it does about Low, me or the readers. Oh Beaverbrook, you should have been alive at that hour…

### Ralph Steadman
*Artist and writer*

'David Low was my *bête noire*. Something turned me off him as the voice of authority. He was what the political cartoon was supposed to look like and others thought so too. Therefore, it was official. I admired his work fearfully but he was just too good. Low was so very clever and maybe that was the problem. Cleverness is the mask of smugness. Too damn clever for his own good.

Low was the insider playing the maverick, hand-in-glove with Lord Beaverbrook. His outrage was a sanctioned protest endorsed by all the good and worthy establishment figures of the time. To be drawn by Low was a seal of approval rather than a criticism. He lacked the truly venal qualities of the great satirists like George Grosz and Otto Dix, John Heartfield and, of course, James Gillray, who got themselves hated by everybody. Otherwise what's the point? You gnash your teeth and march to a populist tune.

He created the foppish attitudes of the modern political cartoon full of its own tired platitudes appealing to a piety that lies dormant in us all. However, I guess someone who simultaneously gets himself hated by the two official great dictators of the 20th century can't be all bad. I was introduced to him when I was hardly 21 and he laughed at my attempts to grow a beard, so maybe it's personal!

## Low's methods and materials

Low mainly used Whatman's 'Hot Pressed' paper, rather than the art board used by most of his contemporaries. He drew the political caricatures in pencil. For his cartoons, he worked with a brush using black and white Indian ink, the latter for corrections. Low used a blue crayon or a blue wash to indicate to the process department where they should apply half-tone. Unlike most cartoonists of his day, Low did not submit roughs to his editor. He worked alone in a studio at 13 Heath Street in Hampstead, refusing to have a telephone or a doorbell. Interviewed for American television in 1959 by Percy Cudlipp, his editor at the *Evening Standard* and the *Daily Herald*, Low stated: '[I] could only produce when left alone, absolutely alone. And, after all, editors and people connected with editors (including yourself, if I may say so) are a damned nuisance. And so I used to have a secret hide-away, with no telephone, no communica-

tions with the outside world. No one used to come to my studio – no one at all… I got free of everyone.'

Low drew a single, very detailed, pencil sketch, which he would then transfer to a clean sheet, spending between five to eight hours on the finished drawing. Low often spent more time taking detail out than putting it in. Someone from the newspaper collected the finished cartoon at about 5.30pm each day. *Tim Benson*

# British Politics during the 1920s and '30s

 &  **Two Liberal Party posters for the 1922 election**

● Posters ● October/November 1922 ● Lent by Low Family

At the 1922 General Election, Low gave his active support to the Liberal Party by drawing a series of election posters for them: '1922 was my first British General Election. I put other things aside and threw myself into it. The *Star* worked closely with Liberal headquarters and we arranged that I would make at least one poster per day. It was probably the last election poster campaign in Britain.'

# The Recruiting Parade

● Cartoon ● First published *Evening Standard*, 7 October 1924 ● Private Collection

With the aid of the Red (Zinoviev) Letter (which apparently showed links between the Soviet Communists and the Labour Party but turned out to be a forgery), Churchill appealed to both Conservatives and Liberals to bring down the first-ever Labour Government. Churchill took Low's cartoons in good light, unlike his friend and colleague Lord Birkenhead (second from right). Churchill remarked in

*Thoughts and Adventures*: 'There is not a figure in it that is not instinct with maliciously perceived truth. Really it is a masterpiece. I showed it to Lord Birkenhead. He had not seen it before. I said cheerfully: "It's astonishing how like you are to your cartoons." FE [Birkenhead] took up the picture... and gazed at it pensively, [then] handed it back to me with the remark: "You seem to be the only one flattered".'

THE RECRUITING PARADE.

## Low arrives at the *Evening Standard*

- Billboard
- Not dated
- Lent by Low Family

Low joined the *Evening Standard* in October 1927 after eight years at the *Star*.

# Opening Day

● Cartoon ● First published *Evening Standard*, 10 October 1927 ● Lent by The House of Commons

When his first image for the *Standard* appeared, Low said, 'I started off with a cartoon displaying characters and symbols and personalities. It went well'. Among the stock characters, Churchill appears as the Napoleonic adventurer. Beneath the figure of Ramsay MacDonald is a rather prophetic sign labelled 'The celebrated Conservative Leader'. Four years later, MacDonald deserted the Labour Government to form a National one, which after the ensuing election was totally dominated by Conservatives. Low always drew MacDonald in court dress because, on becoming Prime Minister of the first Labour Government, he insisted that his somewhat unassuming ministers always wear court dress at state occasions.

OPENING DAY.

# The Hard Lot of a Cartoonist

● Cartoon ● First published *Evening Standard*, 13 October 1927 ● Lent by Beaverbrook Foundation

Low was determined to present himself at the *Evening Standard* as an independent critic. Lord Birkenhead, in particular, quickly came to resent the fact that Lord Beaverbrook had employed Low and, worse still, had given him complete freedom to ridicule even his closest political friends.

Birkenhead's bitterness about Low exploded in a letter he wrote to Beaverbrook: 'As to your filthy cartoonist, I care nothing about him now. But I know about modern caricature and I never had cause for grievance until you, a friend, allowed a filthy little Socialist to present me daily as a crapulous and corpulent buffoon.'

**Top right, left to right:** William Joynson-Hicks, Winston Churchill, Stanley Baldwin (seated), Lord Birkenhead, Austen Chamberlain

THE HARD LOT OF A CARTOONIST.

## Low Howls Down Another Theatrical Production

● Cartoon ● First published *Evening Standard*, 28 November 1927 ● Lent by Beaverbrook Foundation

Four days before this cartoon appeared in the *Evening Standard,* four Labour MPs had been suspended from the House of Commons following stormy scenes arising out of the Conservative Government's tactics over the drastic use of closure on the unemployment insurance bill.

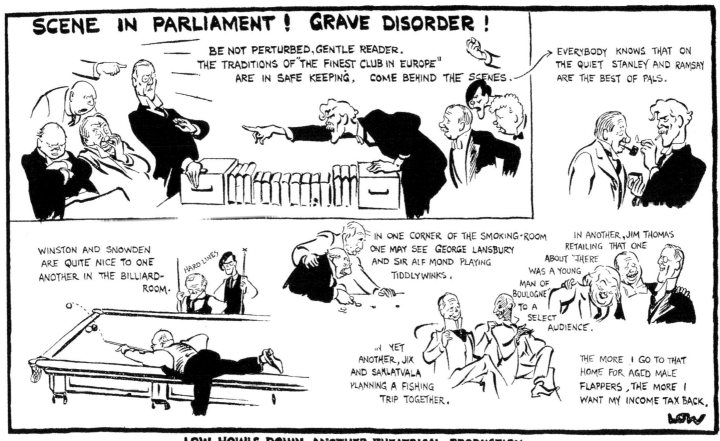

LOW HOWLS DOWN ANOTHER THEATRICAL PRODUCTION.

# Ellen's Mirror of Truth

● Cartoon ● First published *Evening Standard*, 24 March 1928 ● Lent by The House of Commons

Ellen Wilkinson was elected to Parliament in the
General Election of October 1924 as Labour MP for
Middlesborough East, one of the very first women to
enter the male domain of the House of Commons.
Not surprisingly, facilities for women MPs were
almost non-existent.

ELLEN'S MIRROR OF TRUTH.

# 'To facilitate the health of the public mind I would abolish free speech...'

● Cartoon ● First published *Evening Standard*, 26 May 1928 ● Lent by Mrs NJ Ross

Journalist and novelist, Rebecca West, acknowledged as having one of the sharpest wits and most astute minds among her contemporaries, collaborated with David Low on two projects, *Lions and Lambs* in 1928 and *The New Rake's Progress* in 1930, with West writing the commentary for both.

# Illustration from *The Autocracy of Mr Parham* by HG Wells

● Book illustration ● First published Heinemann, 1930 ● Lent by The Political Cartoon Society

*The Autocracy of Mr Parham*, written by HG Wells and illustrated by Low with ten double-page images, was a political satire on the totalitarian tendencies of the time. The character of Mr Parham is an Oxford don taken up by the wealthy and influential, including a tycoon along Beaverbrook lines. A spiritualist séance gives Parham the powers to make himself Lord Paramount of England. In this illustration, we see him dismissing the House of Commons in Cromwellian style. Parham allies England with the fictionalised dictators of other European countries, such as 'Paramuzzi' of Italy. A Second World War quickly follows against the Americans, which leads to them destroying London from the air.

## Between Gandhi and Windhi

● Cartoon ● First published *Evening Standard*, 31 January 1931 ● Lent by The House of Commons

In order to gain India's independence from Britain, Mahatma Gandhi started a campaign of civil disobedience. To highlight the iniquitous tax on salt, Gandhi and his supporters walked across India to the sea where they symbolically tasted untaxed salt. MacDonald, in an attempt to solve the mounting crisis, began a period of conciliation towards the Indian nationalists to which Baldwin, now Leader of the Opposition, offered Conservative support. Churchill's reaction was to resign in indignation from the Conservative Shadow Cabinet, thereby commencing his years in the political wilderness.

BETWEEN GANDHI AND WINDHI.

# In Different Worlds

● Cartoon ● First published *Evening Standard*, 17 April 1934 ● Lent by Beaverbrook Foundation

Neville Chamberlain became the first Chancellor of the Exchequer for five years to have a budget surplus. In what he called his prosperity budget, he took sixpence off income tax but failed to introduce any direct schemes to assist the three million unemployed created by the Depression.

IN DIFFERENT WORLDS.

# Another Ascent Into The Stratosphere

● Cartoon ● First published *Evening Standard*, 11 September 1935 ● Lent by The House of Commons

George Lansbury, leader of the Labour Opposition in the Commons, expressed public disagreement with the Trade Union Congress over its acceptance that the Italian invasion of Abyssinia must be stopped – if necessary by force. By doing this, Lansbury also went against Labour Party policy, which was for collective security through the League of Nations. Ernest Bevin castigated Lansbury, not so much for his pacifism but for his disloyalty to the Labour Party. A month later, Lansbury resigned, to be replaced by Clement Attlee.

ANOTHER ASCENT INTO THE STRATOSPHERE.

# Low's Topical Budget, 1935

- Cartoon
- First published *Evening Standard*, 16 November 1935
- Lent by Beaverbrook Foundation

Low's full page 'Topical Budget' cartoon was published on Saturdays in the *Evening Standard* between 1934 and 1940. This one appeared on the Saturday after the 1935 General Election. It combined both social and political comment. Colonel Blimp appeared in the first Topical Budget on 21 April 1934 and went on to appear regularly in a pocket cartoon along with Low in the bottom right-hand corner. According to Low: 'It began almost as a formula: Colonel Blimp and I at the Turkish bath performing our ablutions or exercising, he uttering to me a blatantly self-contradictory aphorism. It continued in that form with a few exceptions until a war shortage of paper ended my Topical Budget six years later.'

# The Man with Sealed Lips

● Cartoon ● First published *Evening Standard*, 17 February 1936 ● Lent by The House of Commons

Low and Joan Bull, his female counterpart to John Bull, stare at Stanley Baldwin, who had been accused of concealing the need for re-armament before the 1935 General Election. Baldwin explained that his party would have lost the election had he not opposed re-armament. Now, having won, he could go ahead with it. According to Low: 'Torn by a wish to lose neither the favour of the pacifist masses nor chance one day, with a change of wind, to begin a programme of re-armament, Baldwin could not bring himself to trust the people with the full facts of the national position. "My lips are sealed," he said. Whereupon I labelled him Old Sealed Lips, and drew him regularly with gum-tape across his mouth. The nickname spread and I heard that his staff used it at Downing Street.'

THE MAN WITH SEALED LIPS

# Putting Out the Cat

● Cartoon ● First published *Evening Standard*, 14 July 1937 ● Lent by Beaverbrook Foundation

Labour MP Sir Stafford Cripps (glasses, bottom right-hand corner), advocated that the Labour and British Communist Parties should come together to form a 'United Front' against Fascism. Labour leaders, Ernest Bevin (with cat) and Clement Attlee (lying in bed), rejected this and Cripps was eventually expelled from the Labour Party. Seen beside Cripps is Harry Pollitt, Secretary of the Communist Party of Great Britain.

PUTTING OUT THE CAT.

# Today's Special

● Cartoon ● First publication *Evening Standard*, 5 November 1937 ● Lent by Beaverbrook Foundation

Sir John Ganzoni, Chairman of the Kitchen Committee, had made a statement in the House of Commons concerning the presentation of food served at Westminster: 'Some MPs want daintier dishes... They don't like the way the fish is cooked; it always looks and tastes the same. And you should hear what they say about the vegetables.'

Louis Smith, Tory MP for the Hallam Division of Sheffield, also spoke on behalf of other discontented MPs. He suggested that the leading House of Commons chefs should be sent to European cities where he believed they cooked food in a more interesting manner. Smith explained what he though was wrong with House of Commons meals: 'It's monotonous. Fish and vegetables, always the same. Now in other countries, France, for instance, they can cook the same thing in many different ways to make it look and taste better. That's what I'm after – more imagination.' Low uses this story to show Ernest Brown's failure as Minister of Labour to show any imagination whatsoever in alleviating the problem of the unemployed.

**TO-DAY'S SPECIAL.**

# The Abdication Crisis

### Difficult Days for Low

● Cartoon ● First published *Evening Standard*, 9 December 1936 ● Lent by The Political Cartoon Society

This cartoon, drawn during the week that the abdication of King Edward VIII took place, has Low locked in a steam bath by Colonel Blimp, under instruction from Lord Beaverbrook, Low's proprietor. Beaverbrook had 'issued instructions that no cartoons on personalities involved should be published', with the exception, of course, of the Prime Minister. This cartoon may be about the crisis, but it is plainly a tease on Beaverbrook and an admission that the latter had attempted to constrain him.

DIFFICULT DAYS FOR LOW.

# Secretly, in the Dead Of Night

● Cartoon ● First published *Evening Standard*, 11 December 1936 ● Lent by Mr Roger Billis

This cartoon appeared the day after the abdication. Low intended to suggest that the King had been railroaded off the throne by Baldwin (seen here with faceless members of the Establishment), who secretly carries away the throne and crown, while public opinion is gagged. Low is being mischievous here, knowing perfectly well that it was the press barons and not Baldwin who had for so long kept the public ignorant of the crisis. Kenneth Baker holds that this Low cartoon reflected 'the view of his proprietor, Lord Beaverbrook, that the Establishment, led by Baldwin, had knocked the King off the throne against the wishes of the country'. *The Times* believed it was certainly wide of the mark: 'It will be a misfortune if this cartoon is reproduced abroad for it utterly misrepresents the action of the Prime Minister and the response to it of public opinion.'

Beaverbrook later claimed that these two cartoons effectively undermined Baldwin's 'honest broker' image.

SECRETLY, IN THE DEAD OF NIGHT.

 **20**

# Edward, Prince of Wales

● Caricature
● First published *New Statesman*, 1926
● Lent by Mr Reg Bass

In the spring of 1925, while on holiday in France, Low was playing golf one morning when he spotted the Prince playing in a four in front of him, and took the opportunity to sketch him between shots: 'The Prince of Wales was there, a beautiful piece of character in his golf-suit, getting persistently in my line of vision, set up invitingly as a model for me.'

The drawing of the Prince appeared as one of Low's first series of caricatures for the *New Statesman*. Low attracted a certain amount of criticism for drawing the heir to the throne, as he explained in 1935: 'When a few years ago I published a faithful caricature of the Prince of Wales there were the usual squeaks of "Bolshevik".'

# Appeasement and the rise of the Dictators

## The Morning After

● Cartoon ● First published *Evening Standard*, 31 October 1929 ● Lent by Beaverbrook Foundation

On Tuesday 29 October 1929, share prices on the New York Stock Exchange, Wall Street, fell to an all-time low. As a result, thousands of American firms went bankrupt and millions of shareholders were ruined. The American economy nose-dived into the deepest slump in its history.

This cartoon shows Wall Street waking up on the morning after his 'good time' to see the pink rats of financial delirium dancing on the bedrail – the natural result of over-indulgence in the intoxicating spirit of Boom. The portrait of Morgan, Wall Street's patron saint, hangs lopsided on the wall.

THE MORNING AFTER.

# An Ostrich's-Eye View

● Cartoon ● Unpublished ● Lent by The Political Cartoon Society

During the early 1930s, when America was in the throes of a severe economic depression (which was also having a knock-on effect in Europe), Beaverbrook would not accept any cartoon from Low that insinuated the possible downfall of the capitalist system. When Low produced 'An Ostrich's-Eye View', it was refused publication. AJ Cummings, Political Editor of the *News Chronicle*, saw the cartoon in Low's 1936 anthology and, like many others, was amazed that a Low cartoon had been refused publication. Cummings felt that this refusal had had much to do with Beaverbrook:

'Why did this cartoon not appear in the *Evening Standard*? One should be sorry to think it was because Lord Beaverbrook considered it too dangerously Bolshevik.'

AN OSTRICH'S-EYE VIEW.

# Old Low's Almanack – Prophesies for 1931

● Cartoon ● First published *Evening Standard*, 27 November 1930 ● Lent by Beaverbrook Foundation

Eight leading professors and economists were put on trial in the Soviet Union on trumped up charges of not only conspiring to undermine the Soviet economy but also plotting a counter-revolutionary war with support from the British and French. This cartoon offers a prophetic portent of the purges that Stalin inflicted on the Russian people during the 1930s, which resulted in the execution and imprisonment of many millions of innocent people.

# Doormat

● Cartoon ● First published *Evening Standard*, 19 January 1933 ● Lent by Beaverbrook Foundation

In 1931, the Japanese invaded Manchuria, the rich, industrial north-eastern part of China. China and Japan were both members of the League of Nations, and China appealed to it for help. The League set up a Commission of Enquiry, which reported that Japan had had no right to invade China. When the Japanese were ordered to withdraw their troops from Manchuria, they refused and resigned from the League – which then took no further action. In the cartoon we see Sir John Simon, British Foreign Secretary, trying ineffectually to save the League of Nations from a loss of face. By the time this cartoon was published, even the League's strongest supporters had grave doubts about its ability to maintain peace.

THE DOORMAT.

## Barbarism/Civilization

● Cartoon ● First published *Evening Standard*, 11 October 1935 ● Lent by Mr Peter Brookes

Mussolini believed that, like other great nations, Italy should have an empire. Convinced that Britain and France were too fearful of a major war to stop him, Mussolini declared war on Abyssinia (now Ethiopia) on 2 October 1935.

The following day, news reached London of an Italian air-raid on Adowa, the site of Italy's defeat by the Abyssinians in 1896. The first Italian bomb was dropped on a house flying the Red Cross flag and containing hospital stores.

BARBARISM.                    CIVILIZATION.

# 'The Strength of a Chain is that of its Weakest Link'

● Cartoon ● First published *Evening Standard*, 18 October 1935 ● Lent by Beaverbrook Foundation

The League of Nations voted to impose sanctions on Italy after her invasion of Abyssinia. However, the execution of the sanctions policy became a fiasco as oil supplies, crucial to Italy's war effort, were excluded from the forbidden goods. The French Prime Minister Pierre Laval was reluctant to be tough with Mussolini (in tank) in case he was pushed into Hitler's camp. In direct contravention of the League of Nations, Laval (with arm dropped) made an agreement with the British Foreign Secretary, Sir Samuel Hoare, that Italy would be given the northern and southern parts of Abyssinia if she stopped the fighting. Mussolini accepted the Hoare-Laval plan, but in Britain there were protests from those who thought the Plan betrayed Abyssinia. Hoare was forced to resign as Foreign Secretary and the plan abandoned.

"THE STRENGTH OF A CHAIN IS THAT OF ITS WEAKEST LINK."

# 'I demand that German blood be pure' – *Hitler*

● Cartoon ● First published *Evening Standard*, 5 December 1935 ● Lent by Beaverbrook Foundation

In *Mein Kampf*, Hitler wrote: 'All the great civilisations of the past became decadent because the originally creative race died out, as a result of contamination of the blood.' He believed that the most valuable blood, the foundation of a noble race, had been dispersed over the centuries, and aimed to reconstitute the 'blood bank' so Germany could be great again. His racial laws, the concept of the SS as guardians of the new order and the deportation of Jews to concentration camps were all part of his terrible obsession with racial purity. Ironically, none of Nazi Germany's leaders came up to the highest Nazi specifications.

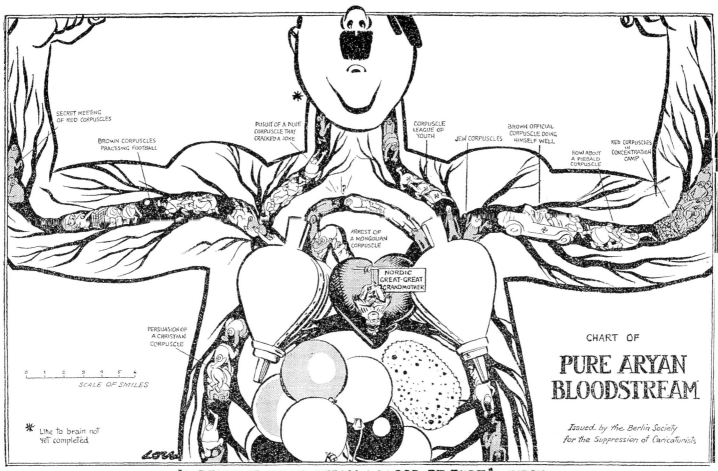

"I DEMAND THAT GERMAN BLOOD BE PURE." — HITLER.

# The Other Fellow with a Funny Moustache

● Cartoon ● First published *Evening Standard*, 14 February 1936 ● Lent by Beaverbrook Foundation

In an allusion to the Charlie Chaplin film, *Modern Times*, Low places the responsibility for the build-up of arms in Europe firmly with Hitler, and emphasises the need for faster re-armament in Britain. This cartoon, like so many by Low, was seen as offensive by the German Foreign Office for the unflattering way in which the Führer was represented.

THE OTHER FELLOW WITH A FUNNY MOUSTACHE.

## Torch of Liberty

- Watercolour
- First published in *Collier's Magazine*
- circa 1937
- Lent by The Political Cartoon Society

In October 1936, Low visited the United States in order, in his words, 'to take a look at eight great American personalities'. They are, from left to right: 'The King of Jazz' Paul Whiteman; journalist and New Dealer Roy Howard; trade union leader John L Lewis; press magnate William Randolph Hearst; Democrat presidential nominee Al Smith; lay preacher Father Divine; former world champion heavyweight boxer Jack Dempsey; and Broadway columnist and broadcaster Walter Winchell.

# Non-intervention Poker

● Cartoon ● First published *Evening Standard*, 13 January 1937 ● Lent by Beaverbrook Foundation

Hitler and Mussolini eventually agreed to the non-intervention scheme. But they failed to comply with it, as Spain was proving a useful training ground for their new armaments and methods of war. The dictators continued to support Franco with troops. Although Hitler sent fewer men than Mussolini, valuable help came from Germany in the form of 11 aircraft squadrons known as the Condor Legion.

TRUSTFUL TONY: "JUST TO DISCOURAGE CHEATING I'LL WEAR A STRAIT-JACKET AND LET YOU BOYS PLAY MY HAND"

NON-INTERVENTION POKER.

# 'You've got to admit I'm bringing peace to the poor suffering Basques'

● Cartoon ● First published *Evening Standard*, 21 June 1937 ● Lent by Prof JM Thoday

In April 1937, the German Condor Legion bombed and destroyed the small Basque town of Guernica in northern Spain, killing over a thousand civilians. The democratic nations were outraged by Franco's treatment of a community that devoutly adhered to the Catholic religion Franco claimed to be defending from barbarism. Rattled, Franco claimed that the people in the 'Red Zone' looked to him for liberation.

" YOU'VE GOT TO ADMIT I'M BRINGING PEACE TO THE POOR SUFFERING BASQUES."

# Standing Room Only

● Cartoon ● First published *Evening Standard*, 30 July 1937 ● Lent by Beaverbrook Foundation

As Hitler stepped up his persecution of the Jews in Germany, growing numbers of Jews looked to emigrate to Palestine. During the First World War, Britain had promised support for both Arab independence and a Jewish National Home in Palestine. A Royal Commission in 1937 reported in favour of partitioning Palestine between Jews and Arabs. Zionist critics objected to the restrictions on immigration and held that the proposed Jewish area was too small, being only one-fifth of Palestine. The British Colonial Secretary, Ormsby-Gore, contended that at least it established a Jewish State.

# Nazi Hunting Exhibition

● Cartoon ● First published *Evening Standard*, 19 November 1937 ● Lent by Beaverbrook Foundation

Lord Halifax accepted an invitation from Goering to attend the International Sporting Exhibition in Berlin. While in Germany, Halifax also held talks with Hitler and with Germany's Propaganda Minister, Goebbels, who explained that Hitler was extremely sensitive to criticism in the British press, especially from English journalists in Berlin and cartoonists. Apparently, Goebbels singled Low out among offending cartoonists. Halifax promised at the end of their meeting that 'the Government would do everything in its power to induce the London Press to avoid unnecessary offence'. When he arrived back in England he immediately contacted the newspapers whose journalists and cartoonists were upsetting Hitler. Halifax confirmed in a letter to the British Ambassador in Berlin, Sir Nevile Henderson, that as far as cartoonists were concerned, Low seemed to be the most vitriolic: 'I am hoping to see the *Daily Herald* and *Daily News* controlling powers [proprietors] myself, but I haven't as yet devised any approach that is satisfactory to Low, who draws the pictures in the *Evening Standard*, and these I expect are the most troublesome of any.'

NAZI HUNTING EXHIBITION.

# Increasing Pressure

● Cartoon ● First published *Evening Standard*, 18 February 1938 ● Lent by Beaverbrook Foundation

Low prophetically anticipated that if Hitler were to succeed in putting pressure on Austria to come under the control of the German Reich, Czechoslovakia (among other European states) would, in turn, go the same way. The cartoon sums up the complacency that still existed in Britain and France at the time. Six months later, Chamberlain, after a second visit to Hitler in an attempt to prevent war over Czechoslovakia, commented: 'How horrible, fantastic, incredible it is that we should be digging trenches and trying on gas masks here because of a quarrel in a far-away country between people of whom we know nothing.'

INCREASING PRESSURE.

# Which backbone shall I lay out this morning, my lord?

● Cartoon ● First published *Evening Standard*, 1 August 1938 ● Lent by Beaverbrook Foundation

When Anthony Eden resigned as Foreign Secretary in February 1938, Chamberlain replaced him with Lord Halifax, who was more in tune with his own ideas on appeasing Hitler and Mussolini. Low thought Halifax a disastrous choice for Foreign Secretary under the circumstances, when in his opinion someone who would take a firm stand with the dictators was needed: 'Lord Halifax was a good and upright man but not quite the right person to deal successfully with persons whose conceptions of goodness and uprightness were the opposite of his own.' Ironically, Hitler would refer to Chamberlain, Daladier and Halifax as 'the spineless worms he had met at Munich' over their acquiescence in his dismantling of Czechoslovakia in autumn 1938.

WHICH BACKBONE SHALL I LAY OUT THIS MORNING. MY LORD ?

# Select Company

● Cartoon ● First published *Evening Standard*, 3 October 1938 ● Lent by The Political Cartoon Society

In what became known as the Munich Agreement, Hitler, Chamberlain, Mussolini and France's Prime Minister Daladier met to decide Czechoslovakia's fate. Neither the Czech President Edouard Benes nor his Russian allies were invited. The four heads of state agreed that Germany should have the Sudetenland (which included most of Czechoslovakia's iron and steel works), with the rest of Czechoslovakia remaining intact. Once again, Hitler had got what he wanted without the need for war. In return, Hitler agreed to sign a note Chamberlain gave him acknowledging that the 'Munich Agreement' was 'symbolic of the desire of our two peoples never to go to war with one another again'. Two days later, Benes (entering from the right) resigned as President of Czechoslovakia. Seven months before, Chancellor Schuschnigg of Austria (in glasses) had also been ousted by Hitler; two years before, Emperor Haile Selassie (with beard) had fled from Ethiopia before Mussolini's armies. The published version omitted Low's text. The cartoon in its original state, shown here, is unambiguous in showing that Low felt the Munich Agreement literally stank, while the edited version appears as just a sad and poignant reflection on what had happened to Benes as a result of Munich.

SELECT COMPANY

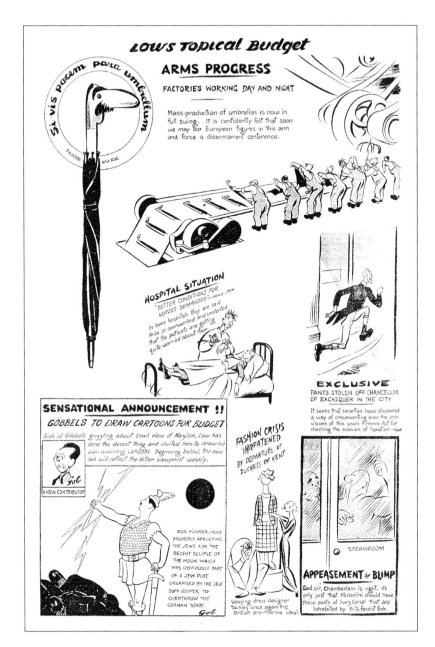

# Topical Budget 1938

- Cartoon
- First published *Evening Standard*, 12 November 1938
- Lent by Beaverbrook Foundation

According to Low: 'Chamberlain was the sort of Englishman who carried his umbrella everywhere. I was struck by its symbolic possibilities. Here could be a new symbol in the ancient tradition of ideographic picture writing, such as the palm for Peace, the clenched fist for Force... [An umbrella] keeps the rain off, shelters from the blast; can lean on it, poke with it, may be blown inside-out, might attract lightning. Perfect. I used the umbrella regularly as a symbol of Chamberlain Appeasement. Sometimes he carried it, sometimes it carried him.'

# Still On The Doorstep

● Cartoon ● First published *Evening Standard*, 5 July 1939 ● Lent by Beaverbrook Foundation

The day this cartoon appeared in the *Evening Standard*, Eden wrote to Churchill noting that 'Low portrays us together on the step of No 10 tonight.' Hitler's invasion of the remnants of Czechoslovakia after the Munich Agreement left Chamberlain's policy of appeasement in tatters – Hitler had now annexed non-German peoples into the Reich. There were soon calls in the press for Churchill's inclusion in the government. He was no longer seen as a warmonger, but as a defender of democracy; the *Daily Mirror* described him as 'Britain's most trusted statesman'. An anonymous supporter paid for a poster to appear in the Strand asking 'What Price Churchill?' However, Chamberlain ignored these requests until the outbreak of war forced his hand.

STILL ON THE DOORSTEP

# Democracy Goes On Holiday

● Cartoon ● First published *Evening Standard*, 4 August 1939 ● Lent by Beaverbrook Foundation

With Hitler expected to invade Poland at any moment, a serious revolt by Tory MPs took place in the House of Commons when the Prime Minister put forward a motion that Parliament should adjourn until 3 October for the summer recess. Chamberlain also astonished the House by declaring that a vote against the Government on this issue would be taken as a vote of no confidence in the Government and against himself in particular. 'I confidently expect my friends to support me,' Chamberlain exclaimed.

DEMOCRACY GOES ON HOLIDAY

# The war years

## Someone Is Taking Someone For A Walk

● Cartoon ● First published *Picture Post*, 2 November 1939 ● Private Collection

On 23 August, the Soviet Union and Nazi Germany shocked the world by signing a non-aggression pact. This opened the way both for Hitler to attack Poland and for Stalin to have a free hand in the Baltic States. By the time this cartoon was published, Poland had been defeated and divided equally between Russia and Germany, who as a result now shared a common border. Low correctly assumed that the pact between these two old adversaries would not last long.

SOMEONE IS TAKING SOMEONE FOR A WALK

# Poland – Lebensraum for the Conquered

● Cartoon ● First published *Picture Post*, 20 January 1940 ● Private Collection

A report that vividly described Nazi atrocities in Poland was presented to the Polish government in exile in Britain on 16 January 1940. Apart from the execution of thousands of Poles, two million Jews and gypsies in Nazi-occupied Poland were suffering the most brutal persecution. This prophetic cartoon offered a terrifying portent of what was to come.

POLAND.—LEBENSRAUM FOR THE CONQUERED

# All Behind You, Winston

● Cartoon ● First published *Evening Standard*, 14 May 1940 ● Private Collection

Churchill replaced Chamberlain as Prime Minister on 10 May 1940, four days after the Germans had begun their invasion of the Low Countries. With Churchill's 'Blood, Toil, Tears and Sweat' speech ringing in his ears, Low captures the drama of what became a defining moment in British History: 'The anguish which infused the great occasions imposed a pregnant simplicity on their interpretation. *All Behind You, Winston* practically drew itself at white heat.'

This became Low's most memorable cartoon of Churchill, expressing the spirit of unity and determination on the formation of his National

Coalition Government. The mood is sombre, but resolute. Low stresses that this is a National Unity government by placing three important Labour figures (Attlee, Bevin and Morrison) next to Churchill. Hugh Dalton patted Churchill on the shoulder and said 'Well done Prime Minister! You ought to get that cartoon of Low, showing us all rolling up our sleeves and falling in behind you, and frame it and stick it up at No 10'. Churchill answered, with a broad grin, 'Yes, that was a good one, wasn't it? He is a darling!' In later years, Churchill was heard to say that this cartoon was Low's greatest of him.

**ALL BEHIND YOU, WINSTON**

# Dunkirk – 'To Fight Another Day'

● Cartoon ● First published *Evening Standard*, 8 June 1940 ● Private Collection

A vast armada of boats, including paddle steamers and pleasure craft from dozens of English coastal holiday resorts, as well as 222 naval vessels, took part in rescuing 338,226 British and French troops from the beaches of Dunkirk despite intense German aerial bombardment and shellfire. Operation Dynamo, the evacuation from Dunkirk, was described by Winston Churchill as 'a miracle of deliverance', and became widely seen in Britain not as a defeat but rather as a morale-boosting victory.

DUNKIRK.—"TO FIGHT ANOTHER DAY"

# 'Very Well, Alone'

● Cartoon ● First published *Evening Standard*, 18 June 1940 ● Lent by Mr John Slessor

After the miracle of Dunkirk, the British did not feel like a defeated people. Even though the French had just capitulated to the Germans, Churchill was determined that Britain would fight on alone.

This cartoon was drawn the day after Churchill's 'finest hour' speech: 'The Battle for France is over... the Battle of Britain is about to begin... Hitler knows that he will have to break us in these islands or lose the war... Let us therefore brace ourselves to our duties and so bear ourselves that, if the British Empire and its Commonwealth lasts for a thousand years, men will still say, "This was their finest hour"' (17 June 1940).

During the Battle of Britain, Lord Beaverbrook gave the cartoon to Sir John Slessor, who was then Air Chief Marshal for Coastal Command. Before the cartoon was given to Slessor it was shown to Winston Churchill, who inscribed it.

"VERY WELL, ALONE"

# Impregnable Target

● Cartoon ● First published *Evening Standard*, 11 September 1940 ● Lent by Madeline Watts

German troops could carry out an invasion only if the Luftwaffe had command of the air. So from July 1940, the Germans launched a series of air attacks against southern England, their target first airfields – then, from September, London.

Low drew this cartoon four days after London had suffered its first major air raid. According to Low,

'Goering's first plan for the Battle of Britain failed, so he changed his tactics and attempted with a series of intensified night raids to bomb London out of action. Londoners coped with the widespread destruction of life and property in a spirit that deserved a share in Churchill's eulogium of "Britain's finest hour".'

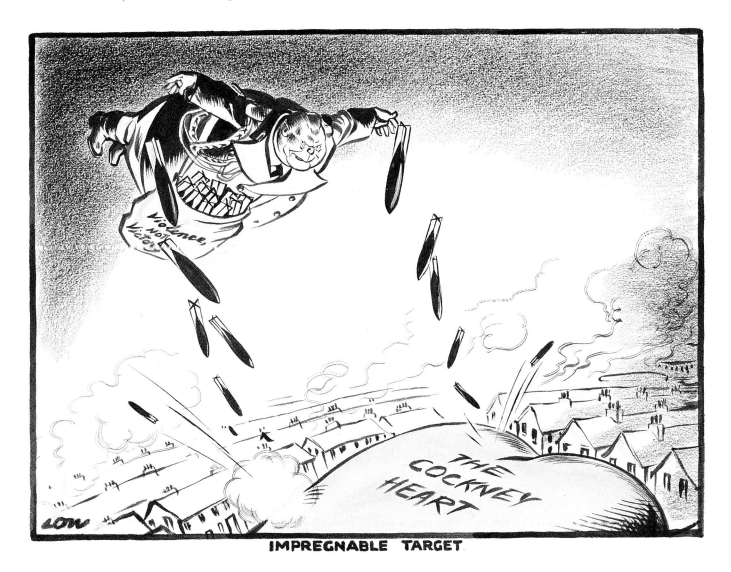

IMPREGNABLE TARGET.

## Sad Tale of a Punctured Chin

● Cartoon ● First published *Evening Standard*, 25 November 1940 ● Lent by New Zealand Cartoon Archive

Mussolini, who dreamed of being Emperor of the Mediterranean, invaded Greece at the end of October 1940 in the belief that his forces would meet little resistance from the Greek army.

Mussolini soon had his pride and confidence punctured when, less than two weeks after crossing the Greek border in great strength, the Italian army was forced to retreat in total disarray.

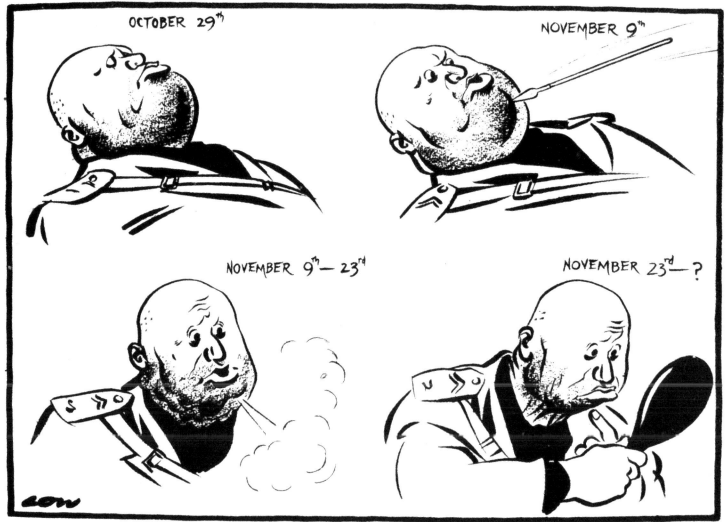

SAD TALE OF A PUNCTURED CHIN

# Battle for Britain – Part 2

● Cartoon ● First published *Evening Standard*, 25 July 1941 ● Lent by Beaverbrook Foundation

After Dunkirk, the Battle of Britain and the threat of imminent invasion had passed, British production started to slow down as public anxiety in Britain lessened. This was also due to the fact that Hitler's attention was now focused on the Soviet Union, which he had attacked on 22 June 1941.

As a result, Low believed: 'The spectacle of Russians and Germans killing one another was viewed with complacent detachment by some die-hard Blimps, in spite of Churchill's warnings that if Russia were conquered there would be very little hope for Britain.'

"IT'S NOT BRITAIN'S WAR, REALLY. IT'S JUST A WAR TO HELP HITLER TO GET WHAT HE NEEDS TO WIPE BRITAIN OUT."

**BATTLE FOR BRITAIN — PART 2.**

# In Occupied Territory

● Cartoon ● First published *Evening Standard*, 10 July 1942 ● Lent by Beaverbrook Foundation

Hitler's code of conduct for the conquering Germans emphasised the necessity of extreme ruthlessness. Yet, although his own relations with his quislings and puppet rulers were said in Berlin to be 'marked by the spirit of cordial friendship', the Führer complained frequently of the lack of appreciation of his high motives among the conquered peoples.

IN OCCUPIED TERRITORY

# Imperial Welcome

● Cartoon ● First published *Evening Standard*, 7 September 1943 ● Lent by Beaverbrook Foundation

This is one of the earliest cartoons to attack colour discrimination. Learie Constantine, a member of the West Indian cricket side (who had lived mainly in Lancashire since 1929) was refused entry to a hotel in London's West End because white American troops were staying there at the time. American troops were segregated throughout the Second World War. Among later distinctions, Constantine became the first black life peer.

IMPERIAL WELCOME

# House of Cards

● Cartoon ● First published *Evening Standard*, 25 August 1944 ● Lent by Beaverbrook Foundation

On the day the Allies liberated Paris, the German position in the Balkans collapsed like a house of cards. Rumania, which had fought on the side of Germany, declared war on its former ally, while Bulgaria announced its intention to withdraw from the war altogether. According to Low, 'Hitler had used up the satellite states, and when his power weakened he had no support among their peoples.'

**HOUSE OF CARDS**

# The whole German people should be wiped out for this!

● Cartoon ● First published *Evening Standard*, 19 April 1945 ● Lent by The Political Cartoon Society

The sickening horrors exposed by the liberation of concentration camps such as Dachau, Buchenwald and Belsen by the Allies shocked the whole world. Drawn the week these camps were liberated, this cartoon was highly controversial as it implied that not all Germans could be held responsible for what had happened. Low points out that those who were happy to blame immediately and indiscriminately all Germans had to be reminded of the hundreds of thousands of Germans who had also suffered and died in these camps for their opposition to Hitler. On the day the Allies liberated Paris, the German position in the Balkans collapsed like a house of cards. Rumania, which had fought on the side of Germany, declared war on its former ally, while Bulgaria announced its intention to withdraw from the war altogether. According to Low, 'Hitler had used up the satellite states, and when his power weakened he had no support among their peoples.'

## Colonel Blimp

*Blimp (blimp); 1. Small non-rigid air-ship. 2. Colonel Blimp, character invented by the cartoonist David Low (b.1891) representing a pompous, obese, elderly figure popularly interpreted as a type of diehard or reactionary. Hence Blimpery or Blimpishness.*
*The Concise Oxford Dictionary, 1964*

David Low got the idea for Colonel Blimp after over-hearing 'two pink sweating chaps of military bearing' in a Turkish bath agreeing that if horses had to go as a consequence of the mechanisation of the cavalry, troops should still be entitled to wear their spurs inside tanks. 'I decided to invent a "character",' Low wrote years later, 'typifying the current disposition to mixed-up thinking, to having it both ways, to dogmatic doubleness, to paradox and plain self-contradiction.' On 21 April 1934, Colonel Blimp made his first appearance in Low's full page Saturday 'Topical Budget' in the *Evening Standard* (see cartoon number 14 for the 'Topical Budget' of 1934).
In 1943, the British film-makers Michael Powell and Emeric Pressburger made *The Life and Death of Colonel Blimp*. The film highlighted the limitations that Britain faced in fighting a modern war with the out-dated methods associated with Colonel Blimp. Winston Churchill saw the project as an attack on the morale of the British Army's officer corps. Seeing the film as propaganda in support of the enemy, he did his utmost to have it banned. For all Churchill's anxieties, the suspected exposé of the Blimpishness alive and well in British high command was all rather muted.

 **This England**
- Magazine cover illustration
- First published *New Statesman and Nation*, December 1939
- Lent by Prof Peter Mellini

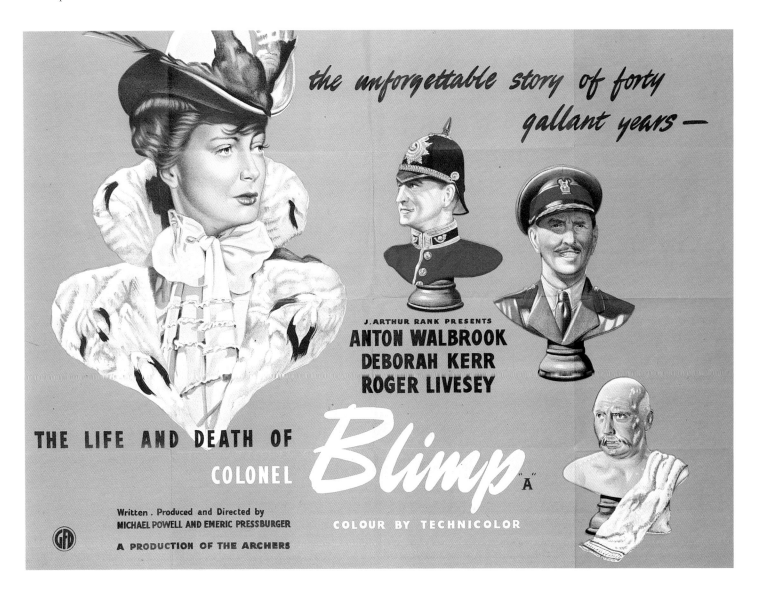

# Post-war Britain

## 54 Diogenes Election Tour

● Cartoon ● First published *Evening Standard*, 29 May 1945 ● Lent by Beaverbrook Foundation

Low cocks a snook at his own employer, Lord Beaverbrook, by emphasising his freedom of comment at the *Evening Standard* about the coming general election. His retreat into a barrel is a reference to the Cynic philosopher Diogenes, who lived in a barrel and was allowed considerable latitude for comment by ancient Athenians. Low shows Britain being wrapped up and presented to Winston Churchill, the Prime Minister, as a gift for winning the war. The temptation for the Tories to fight the election on the strength of Churchill's personality was too strong to ignore. His personal popularity was enormous; the huge crowds that cheered him at every point on his election tours confirmed this. However, the Conservative Party was deeply unpopular, remembered as it was for its attempts to appease Hitler and its inability to deal with the high unemployment of the 1930s.

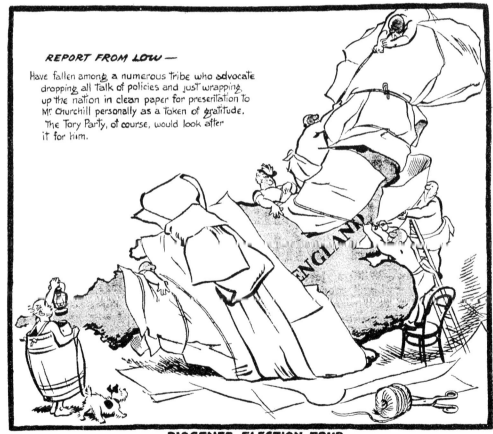

REPORT FROM LOW —

Have fallen among a numerous tribe who advocate dropping all talk of policies and just wrapping up the nation in clean paper for presentation to Mr Churchill personally as a token of gratitude. The Tory Party, of course, would look after it for him.

**DIOGENES ELECTION TOUR**

# Continuity of Foreign Policy

● Cartoon ● First published *Evening Standard*, 30 July 1945 ● Lent by Beaverbrook Foundation

The July 1945 general election was a humiliating defeat for the Tories. Attlee became Prime Minister of a Labour Government that had a majority over all other parties for the first time in its history. Attlee and his Foreign Secretary Ernest Bevin replaced Churchill and Eden at the conference table at Potsdam. The Russians were mystified by their presence; Molotov could not understand why Churchill had not 'fixed' the election. Low's caption, 'Continuity of Foreign Policy', was an accurate assessment, as the then American Secretary of State James Byrnes noted: 'Britain's stand before the Potsdam Conference was not altered in the slightest, so far as one could discern by the replacements'. This led one Labour MP to remark of Bevin, 'Hasn't Anthony Eden grown fat?'

CONTINUITY OF FOREIGN POLICY

# Two Churchills

● Cartoon ● First published *Evening Standard*, 31 July 1945 ● Private Collection

The British people rejected Churchill as a peacetime Prime Minister, but applauded him as the man who had won the war. This memorable cartoon, according to historian Joseph Darracott, 'fuses a personal and popular view of Churchill, while at the same time making an acute historical judgement. This judgement is a historical event and the cartoon cannot be bettered as a way of remembering the British electorate's gratitude to Churchill in the war years, and its distrust of the Conservative Party and its policies'.

Attlee had suggested, after Churchill's 'Gestapo' speech, that he must have wanted to show the voters 'how great was the difference between Winston Churchill, the great leader in war, and Mr Churchill the party leader'. Clementine Churchill tried to ease the blow of her husband's election defeat by commenting that it may have been a blessing in disguise, to which he quickly retorted, 'At the moment it seems quite effectively disguised.'

# New Public Relations Office at 10 Downing St

● Cartoon ● First published *Evening Standard*, 5 October 1945 ● Lent by Beaverbrook Foundation

Low draws himself presenting alternative images of Prime Minister Clement Attlee to the new Press Officer at No 10, Francis Williams, in order to help improve the PM's lacklustre image with the public. Attlee was, like his public persona, a quiet and mild-mannered man. On occasions, Winston Churchill made humorous capital out of this by referring to Attlee as 'a sheep in sheep's clothing' or 'a modest man with much to be modest about'. Attlee was also a notoriously difficult interviewee, frequently replying to questions from journalists with the one-word answer 'yes' or 'no'.

Low also found Attlee's lack of personality frustrating: 'I had never been able to get to know Attlee more than slightly, which accounted for my failure to extract his essence. My impression of him was of a tight-buttoned little man, shy of ridicule. Someone had told him I was an Australian, so whenever we met he confined the conversation to cricket, about which I knew nothing.'

NEW PUBLIC RELATIONS OFFICE AT 10 DOWNING ST.

# United Surgery in Germany

● Cartoon ● First published *Evening Standard*, 26 October 1945 ● Lent by Dr YR Mayhew

Under the Potsdam agreement dismembered Germany was to be de-militarised and de-industrialised to prevent a war of revenge, and then administered as one economic whole. But its main food-producing area was already incorporated into Poland, together with the Silesian industrial belt; if its heavy industry in the west were to be dismantled, firstly the Germans would have no means of support, and secondly Europe would be deprived of production necessary for recovery. The French held that the safest course would be to postpone centralising the administration and to incorporate the Ruhr and Rhineland industries into Western Europe. Moscow complained that this was an anti-Russian idea because it would vastly cut reparations. Washington disliked it for different reasons. But the problem remained.

UNITED SURGERY IN GERMANY

# 'I'll attend to the foundations later'

● Cartoon ● First published *Evening Standard*, 9 October 1946 ● Lent by Beaverbrook Foundation

No one within the Labour Government was prepared to tell trade union bosses that the standard of living for their members was likely to fall while reconstruction was being carried out. Nor were they told that they would have to work harder in future to maintain even their existing standards. Sir Stafford Cripps (Chancellor of the Exchequer), Clement Attlee (Prime Minister) and Herbert Morrison (Lord President of the Council) look on, bemused.

"I'LL ATTEND TO THE FOUNDATIONS LATER"

# 'What! Foreigners? In <u>our</u> country?'

● Cartoon ● First published *Evening Standard*, 12 February 1947 ● Lent by Charles Reiss

In contrast to pre-war unemployment, labour was in short supply during the late 1940s. Consequently, 10,000 Poles, many of whom had fought alongside the British during the war, along with Italian and German ex-PoWs, were allowed to take up residence in England to fill the vacancies in the jobs market. There was criticism from some quarters that these foreigners would take jobs away from Britons. Current attitudes towards asylum seekers may echo this cartoon.

WHAT! FOREIGNERS? IN <u>OUR</u> COUNTRY?

# Micawber's Family Conference

● Cartoon ● First published *Evening Standard*, 2 October 1947 ● Lent by Beaverbrook Foundation

Low deplored Churchill's refusal during the whole of Labour's term in office to be pinned down on specific policy. Churchill would only repeat that he would wait and see what the economic circumstances were at the time of the next election. Consequently, Low created 'Micawber' Churchill who was 'waiting for something to turn up'. Many felt that Low had now gone too far. There was immediate uproar among *Evening Standard* readers, who filled the letters pages denouncing Low's ridicule of such a great man. Under pressure the Editor announced: 'What shall we do with Low?' 'Send him back to New Zealand!' was the response from one retired Admiral.

MICAWBER'S FAMILY CONFERENCE

# Un-American Activities

● Cartoon ● First published *Evening Standard*, 24 August 1948 ● Lent by Beaverbrook Foundation

As Communism grew stronger after 1945, many Americans feared that there were 'Reds' in their country in positions of power and able to undermine their government. A senator from Wisconsin, Joseph McCarthy, seized on these fears and began a search for Communists that became known as a witch-hunt. McCarthy forced people to appear before the Committee of Un-American Activities, under the auspices of which he bullied government officials, writers, businessman and even Hollywood film stars into admitting that they were Communists. Even though being a Communist was not against the law, an appearance before McCarthy was normally enough to lose someone their job and even their friends.

# 'Look at them! Gnashing our own teeth at us!'

● Cartoon ● First published *Evening Standard*, 1 April 1949 ● Lent by Beaverbrook Foundation

It was natural that while Marshall Aid and the North Atlantic Pact were costing the US so much, Americans should be interested in what happened to their dollars. Opponents of the Truman Government in America, assisted by opponents of the Attlee government in Britain, offered as gospel truth wildly exaggerated statements about the British 'Welfare State' and National Health plan, especially such picturesque details as the providing of false teeth and wigs. The implication was that all this was being subsidised by the American taxpayer. 'Baldies' below with wigs include Beaverbrook, Attlee, Blimp and Low himself.

# What a Headache Sometimes To Be With America

● Cartoon ● First published *Daily Herald*, 12 January 1951 ● Lent by The Political Cartoon Society

Low, like many in the Labour Party, was uncertain about taking America's side in the Cold War. The wild speeches of some American politicians suggesting the settlement of disputes with Russia and China by dropping atomic bombs on them made moderate British public opinion fearful and uneasy. On the other hand, when the British looked towards Stalin's Soviet Union, they feared that without the support of America the outlook would be bleak indeed. At least the Americans carried out their witch-hunts in public.

# World Citizen

From September 1951, Low drew a cartoon strip for the *Daily Herald* called 'World Citizen'. It featured Low's 'common man' who, at the height of the Cold War, found himself one day a victim of McCarthyism and the next, perhaps, being purged by the Soviet Secret Police. World Citizen lived in a world of ideologies, austerities, production targets, and the growing threat of atomic warfare.

According to Low: 'Since my hero is a World Citizen, place and distance will have no problems for him. He will pop up when necessity arises in Britain, America, Asia and Europe before and behind the Iron Curtain, getting himself complicated in the troubles of life under all systems: Fascism, Communism and Democracy. I hope he will demonstrate that alongside tragedy always lies comedy – even farce.'

## World Citizen: Champion Worker

- Watercolour
- First published *Daily Herald*, 29 October 1951
- Lent by The Political Cartoon Society

## World Citizen: Confession Drug

- Cartoon
- First published *Daily Herald*, 10 March 1952
- Lent by The Political Cartoon Society

## World Citizen: Anti-Red Witch-Hunt

● Cartoon ● First published *Daily Herald*, 22 November 1951 ● Lent by The Political Cartoon Society

## World Citizen: Ideologies and Reality

● Cartoon ● First published *Daily Herald*, 26 March 1952 ● Lent by The Political Cartoon Society

# Background

● Cartoon ● First published *The Guardian*, 30 May 1953 ● Lent by The Political Cartoon Society

Published three days before the coronation of Queen Elizabeth II, Low emphasises the historical background behind Britain's constitutional monarchy. Behind the throne is a figure representing the British people holding an orb (symbolising Law) and a sceptre (for Parliament). On the right-hand side of this figure we see a number of recognisable historical personages who have made their own significant contribution to British democracy through time: King John with the Magna Carta in his hand; Oliver Cromwell; William the Conqueror; Herbert Asquith; and Lloyd George.

BACKGROUND

# 'Just a lot of Un-Americans'

● Cartoon ● First published *The Guardian*, 10 November 1954 ● Lent by The Political Cartoon Society

McCarthyism eventually imploded. Senator McCarthy's big mistake was to hold hearings seeking Communists in the US Army, and hold them on national television. Thousands of Americans saw for the first time how he bullied witnesses, and how ridiculous his accusations were. It was impossible to believe McCarthy's claims that the US Army fighting the Communist North Koreans was riddled with Communists itself. The Senate became highly critical of McCarthy, and closed down the Un-American Activities Committee. The McCarthy witch-hunts were over.

"JUST A LOT OF UN-AMERICANS"

# Churchill's Eightieth Birthday

● Watercolour ● First published *Illustrated*, 19 November 1954 ● Private Collection

Commissioned by *Illustrated* to draw a commemorative cartoon for an eightieth birthday edition, Low painted a cartoon featuring a room packed with Winston Churchills, all at different stages of his long and eventful life. Signed 'from your old castigator', the original cartoon was presented by the Houses of Parliament to Sir Winston. He was delighted with it, unlike his official present, a portrait by Graham Sutherland, which his wife later destroyed.

# Early Spring Clean

● Cartoon ● First published *The Guardian*, 20 March 1956 ● Lent by The Political Cartoon Society

Nikita Khrushchev finally became Soviet leader following two years of 'collective leadership' after Stalin's death in March 1953. In a speech at the Twentieth Congress of the Communist Party, Khrushchev shocked his audience by bitterly attacking Stalin's rule. He ruthlessly exposed Stalin's excesses and mistakes and accused him of 'flagrant abuses of power and of brutality for the mass arrests [of the purges] which caused tremendous harm to our country and to the cause of Socialist progress'. On an optimistic note, Khrushchev also stressed that he was looking for peaceful co-existence and better relations with the West.

EARLY SPRING CLEAN

# Low's Guide To The World – Alabama, USA

● Cartoon ● First published *The Guardian*, 28 February 1956 ● Lent by The Political Cartoon Society

On 5 December 1955, Rosa Parks, a black, middle-aged seamstress in Montgomery, Alabama, refused to give up her seat to a white man when ordered to by a bus driver. She was arrested and charged with breaking Montgomery's segregation laws, one of the many 'Jim Crow' pieces of legislation in the southern states of the USA that racially segregated buses, waiting rooms and hotels, and prevented many black people from voting. To show solidarity, the black community in the city boycotted the buses when Rosa Parks appeared in court. Found guilty, she refused to pay the $14 fine. After the verdict, the Montgomery Improvement Association (MIA) was born. Its president, a 26-year-old church minister named Martin Luther King, said 'We are tired of being kicked about by the brutal feet of oppression.' The boycott continued and King emphasised its non-violent nature: 'The only weapon that we have in our hands is the weapon of protest.' Financial support flooded in from around the world and MIA developed its own free transport service. Black people walked miles rather than use the white-owned buses. Eventually the US Supreme Court ruled the bus segregation unconstitutional; a major early victory for the civil rights movement.

87

# 'Me, Too!'

● Cartoon ● First published *The Guardian*, 6 November 1956 ● Lent by The Political Cartoon Society

In July 1956, Egypt's Colonel Gamal Abd al-Nasser nationalised the Suez Canal in retaliation for the decision by the Americans not to fund the building of a dam at Aswan. The British Prime Minister, Anthony Eden (in pilot's helmet), believed Nasser was another Hitler, out to expand and rule the entire Middle East. Eden felt that dictators should be brought to heel sooner rather than later. Consequently, in November, British and French forces secretly collaborated with Israel in a military action to regain control of the Canal. The operation was a success, but world condemnation was so great that the British and French had to withdraw and leave the United Nations to pick up the pieces. Russian leader Nikita Khrushchev took the Suez invasion as cover for his own attack on Hungary.

"ME, TOO!"

# 'People's Democracy'

● Cartoon ● First published *The Guardian*, 13 November 1956 ● Lent *by* The Political Cartoon Society

On 1 November 1956 the Hungarian people attempted to overthrow the pro-Soviet regime in Budapest. They demanded an end to the Stalinist system that had been imposed on them, and called for free elections, which would probably mean the end of Communism in Hungary. This was too much for the Russians; if other Soviet satellite states followed suit, Russia's buffer zone against the West would evaporate.

On 4 November, taking advantage of the Suez Crisis in the Middle East, Khrushchev sent 6,000 Russian tanks rumbling into Hungary in order to crush the uprising. This they did, killing 30,000 Hungarians in the process. A new Soviet-backed government was installed. None of the Western powers came to Hungary's aid.

"PEOPLE'S DEMOCRACY"

# Final Test of Greatness

● Cartoon ● First published *The Guardian*, 26 July 1957 ● Lent by The Political Cartoon Society

The House of Commons, on a motion by Sir Winston Churchill, authorised a memorial statue to David Lloyd George, who died in 1945. Sir Jacob Epstein was commissioned to make it. Low shows a horrified Lloyd George, accompanied by two angels, obviously deeply concerned with how the finished work would turn out at the hands of this great modernist sculptor.

Epstein died in August 1959, before he was able to complete the sculpture, and it was finished by Uli Nimptsch. On 18 December 1963, the statue, which stands in the Members' Lobby outside the doorway into the House of Commons debating chamber, was unveiled by Prime Minister Sir Alec Douglas-Home.

FINAL TEST OF GREATNESS

# 'In the name of Africa (ahem!) welcome!'

● Cartoon ● First published *The Guardian*, 5 January 1960 ● Lent by The Political Cartoon Society

A large proportion of Africa had been colonised by European countries by the beginning of the twentieth century. On the day this cartoon was published, Prime Minster Harold Macmillan left for a tour of African States. It was during this tour that Macmillan angered members of the South African parliament when he declared in Cape Town: 'In the twentieth century we have seen the awakening of national consciousness in peoples who have lived for centuries in dependence on some other power. Fifteen years ago this movement spread through Asia.

Many countries there, of different races and civilisations, pressed their claims to an independent national life. Today the same thing is happening in Africa. The most striking of all the impressions I have formed since I left London a month ago is of the strength of this African national consciousness. In different places it may take different forms, but it is happening everywhere. The wind of change is blowing through this continent and, whether we like it or not, this growth of national consciousness is a political fact.'

"IN THE NAME OF AFRICA (AHEM!) WELCOME!"

# Question Time

- Cartoon
- First published *The Guardian*, 17 February 1960
- Lent by Low Family

Macmillan returned from his tour of Africa to be confronted by angry Tory backbenchers, alarmed at the possible ramifications of his 'Winds of Change' speech in South Africa. In protest, many had rejected proposals for Kenyan independence set out by the Colonial Secretary, Iain Macleod. Here, behind Macmillan and a front bench of future African leaders, the wraiths of Blimps protest in vain.

QUESTION TIME

# History Repeats Itself

● Cartoon ● First published *The Guardian*, 29 May 1960 ● The Political Cartoon Society

The Labour Party had decided to re-examine its H-Bomb policy. The Labour shadow defence minister George Brown indicated in the Commons that Labour might withdraw its support for an independent nuclear deterrent. At the Labour Party Conference in Scarborough, a resolution calling for unilateral nuclear disarmament was pushed through. Hugh Gaitskell, the Labour Party leader (in black, juxtaposed with the shade of George Lansbury, Labour's pacifist leader in the 1930s), responded with a famous speech in which he promised to 'fight and fight and fight again' to overturn this decision 'and save the party we love'.

# Drive to Next Election

● Cartoon ● First published *The Guardian*, 15 July 1960 ● Lent by The Political Cartoon Society

The Labour Leader, Hugh Gaitskell, reacted to his party's third election defeat in a row in 1959 by demanding that Clause Four be dropped from the party's constitution. Clause Four committed Labour to the common ownership of the means of production, distribution and exchange. A furious debate began amongst the party faithful, with many seeing Gaitskell's intentions as a betrayal of their socialist ideals. The Labour Party eventually abandoned Clause Four in 1995, under a new leader, Tony Blair.

**DRIVE TO NEXT ELECTION**

# What, Again?

● Cartoon ● First published *The Guardian*, 12 September 1961 ● Lent by The Political Cartoon Society

Speaking at a ceremony in Stalingrad, the Soviet leader Khrushchev warned that while a nuclear war would not totally destroy a vast nation like Russia, it could destroy countries such as Britain, France and West Germany, which had much more dense populations. This was Khrushchev's second threatening reference to Britain within a few days; he had told an interviewer that fear of being wiped out would keep the British out of a future conflict between the Soviet bloc and the United States.

WHAT, AGAIN ?

# Camel and Eye of Needle

● Cartoon ● First published *The Guardian*, 13 October 1961 ● Lent by The Political Cartoon Society

Doubts in Europe over Britain's applying to join the Common Market were dissipated when Edward Heath, Lord Privy Seal, addressed the French Foreign Ministry. Heath stated that the British Government would accept the Treaty of Rome. A debate took place at the Conservative Party Conference in Brighton about the Common Market. Here Low shows Tory pro-Europeans Heath (with needle) and RA Butler (in Arab robe) trying to persuade Tory hardliners mounted on a Blimpish camel to go through the eye of the European needle.

**CAMEL AND EYE OF NEEDLE**

## 'Show me first'

● Cartoon ● First published *The Guardian*, 8 June 1962 ● Lent by The Political Cartoon Society

During a debate in the House of Commons on the Common Market, both Hugh Gaitskell (with stick) and his spokesman on foreign affairs, Harold Wilson (far left), called upon Edward Heath (right) to 'come clean' and reveal the government's proposals for Britain's entry into the EEC, about which the Labour Party was then unenthusiastic. In the autumn of 1962, Gaitskell announced at the Labour Party conference that entry into the EEC would 'mean the end of a thousand years of British history'.

"SHOW ME FIRST"

# Low's caricatures

According to David Low, 'A caricature is a drawing based upon the truths of the subject, in which those salient points which give character are especially emphasised. For instance, the Sunday-school teacher's expression on the face of Sir John Simon, with which the meditative bend of the neck, the rounded shoulders and the clasped hands are in common harmony. A good caricaturist brings out those character points; a bad artist might caricature a man without noticing anything of a distinctive nature.' Low produced two series of caricatures for the *New Statesman* in 1926 and 1933 respectively. These appeared as a loose supplement in the magazine. Lord Beaverbrook, after viewing the complete first series, considered that Lloyd George and Snowden were the best 'and that of Winston is too cruel'. In 1952, Low produced another fifty caricatures for a book called *Low's Company*.

## First series

## Ramsay MacDonald (1866-1937)

● First published *New Statesman*, 23 January 1926 ● Lent by Low Family

Labour MP for Leicester (1906-1918), Aberavon (1922-35), Scottish Universities (1935-37); Prime Minister (1924, 1929-35).
Low: I was perhaps too greatly impressed by Ramsay MacDonald, who looked to me a real leader. He seemed taller in those days and more craggy, as he stalked up and down. A handsome figure, fine voice, shabby blue serge suit, handlebar moustache, solid black against solid white of hair forelock. I enjoyed drawing him. Although I had him out of all proportion, physically and otherwise, I didn't know it. For many years he was to be one of my failures in representation, until I outgrew that windswept-hero first impression.

# Sir William Joynson-Hicks (1865-1937)

- First published *New Statesman*, 20 February 1926
- Lent by The Political Cartoon Society

Conservative MP for Brentford; Minister for Health (1923-24), Home Secretary (1924-29); First Viscount Brentford (1929). Joynson-Hicks, nicknamed 'Jix', was a notably reactionary Conservative Home Secretary. Low: 'Jix was a joy to draw, with his small lined face with the tiny snub nose… When the elaborate portrait arising from [his] first sitting at last appeared in print, it displayed him in Napoleonic attitude, dressed in the full glory of his habitual outfit as the Complete Statesmen, Victorian vintage, with choker collar and silk-faced frock coat.'

# David Lloyd George (1863-1945)

- First published *New Statesman*, 6 March 1926
- Lent by Low Family

Liberal MP for Caernarfon; Chancellor of the Exchequer (1908-15), Minister of Munitions (1915-16), Prime Minister (1916-22).

Low: 'I always had the greatest difficulty in making LG sinister in a cartoon. Every time I drew him, however critical the comment, I had to be careful or he would spring off the drawing-board a lovable cherubic little chap.'

# Sir Austen Chamberlain (1863-1937)

● First published *New Statesman*, 20 March 1926,
● Lent by The Political Cartoon Society

Conservative MP for East Worcestershire (1892-1914), West Birmingham (1914-37); Chancellor of the Exchequer (1903-05, 1919-21); Foreign Secretary (1924-29). Followed his father Joseph Chamberlain (1837-1914) in wearing a monocle, orchid, wing collar and frock coat. Half brother of Neville. The only Leader of the Conservative Party (until William Hague) never to become Prime Minister.

Lord Birkenhead said of Austen Chamberlain: 'He always played the game and he always lost it.'

Low: 'Austen Chamberlain was the very apotheosis of English starchy stiffness. A mutual friend had arranged an interview. It was just after the Locarno Pact and the Foreign Secretary was said to be in a good mood. Half-way down the spacious room at the Foreign Office was a table upon which rested the silk hat and the yellow gloves. In the distance stood what I thought at first was a statue.

"I have been asking myself how I should receive you," it said, showing minute signs of life.

"Well then, don't receive me at all. Pretend I'm not here," I said.

"Must I wear my monocle? I cannot see to read with it very well…"

"Yes, you should wear your monocle." It was a valuable tag of identity so far as I was concerned.'

LOW

Sir Austen

## Max Aitken, First Lord Beaverbrook (1879-1964)

- First published *New Statesman*, 27 March 1926
- Lent by Mr and Mrs GG Walker

Conservative MP for Ashton-under-Lyne (1910-17);
Peer 1917. As well as the *Evening Standard*,
Beaverbrook acquired a controlling interest in the
*Daily Express*. In 1940, Churchill brought Beaverbrook
into his War Cabinet where he served as Minister for
Aircraft Production (1940-41); Minister of Supply
(1941-42); Minister of War Production (1942) and
Lord Privy Seal (1943-45).
Lord Beaverbrook's friend and biographer, AJP Taylor
wrote: 'The best likeness is the famous drawing by
Low, though it makes Beaverbrook misleadingly
small.' According to Low: 'The fact that Lord
Beaverbrook talks into the telephone like a man
10 feet high represents an essential quality which in
the expression of his real self is of more importance
than the actual fact about his height.'

Max, Lord Beaverbrook.

# Philip Snowden (1864-1937)

● First published *New Statesman*, 3 April 1926
● Lent by The Political Cartoon Society

Labour MP for Blackburn (1906-18), Colne Valley (1922-31); Chancellor of the Exchequer (1924, 1929-31); Peer 1931.

According to Low: 'Snowden was one of the generation of socialists whose historic purpose was to inspire – to create an atmosphere. A reformer, not a revolutionary. When it came to doing anything – finding ways and means – he always looked to me like a radical Liberal, treating socialism as an attitude for the individual rather than as a public policy. Hence developments like the "iron-jawed Chancellor" of financial orthodoxy when he was in office, the "correctness" of his attitude to the financial crisis of 1931, and the conventional free-trader's indignation with which he flounced out of the National Government shortly after.'

Philip Snowden

# Sir Winston Spencer Churchill (1874-1965)

● First published *New Statesman*, 1 May 1926
● Lent by the British Museum

Conservative MP for Oldham (1900-06), Liberal MP for
North West Manchester (1906-22), Conservative MP
for Epping (1924-64); President of the Board of Trade
(1908-10), Home Secretary (1910-11), First Lord of the
Admiralty (1911-15), Minister of Munitions (1917-18),
Minister of War and Air (1919-20), Colonial Secretary
(1921-22), Chancellor of the Exchequer (1924-29),
Prime Minister (1940-45, 1951-55).

Low: 'Churchill in the flesh belonged to that sandy
type which cannot be rendered properly in black
lines. His eyes, blue, bulbous and heavy lidded,
would be impossible. The best one could do with
them would be an approximation. At this time all the
political cartoonists were using the approximation
worked out by ET Reed, the *Punch* caricaturist, who
was feeling a bit disgruntled about the plagiarism.
"That fellow," Reed complained to me about a
colleague, "he's a thief. He stole my Winston's eye."'

## Frederick Edwin Smith, First Earl of Birkenhead (1872-1930)

● First published *New Statesman*
● Lent by Mr Jeremy K Benson

Conservative MP for Liverpool Walton; Solicitor General (1915), Attorney General (1915-19), Lord Chancellor (1919-22), Secretary of State for India (1924-28). Peer 1922.

A brilliant lawyer, noted for his cruel wit. Close friend of Churchill. Low nicknamed him 'Lord Burstinghead', because he never attempted to conceal his superior brainpower and his contempt for the Labour Party. His friends demanded, 'seriously and quite regardless of the point', according to Low, that he amend the soubriquet to 'Bestinhead'. Low declined.

Lord Birkenhead.

# James H Thomas (1874-1949)

● First published *New Statesman*, 10 July 1926
● Lent by the National Portrait Gallery

Labour MP for Swindon (1910-31), National Labour
MP for Derby (1931-36); Secretary of State for the
Colonies (1924, 1931-36), Lord Privy Seal (1929-31).
During Labour's first period in office (1924), Low
often saw Thomas hobnobbing with members of the
House of Lords in full evening dress. Low therefore
drew Thomas as The Right Hon. Dress Suit MP, a
symbol of the new respectibility of the Labour Party.
Low: 'Thomas was a friendly soul and I saw him
often. "I will hand you down to posterity, Jimmy,"
I said to him. "You don't 'and me down to posterity,
David, you 'ound me down," says he. While my mail
filled with angry letters from readers accusing me of
gross assault on Thomas's dignity, there were very
few cartoons about him that were not followed by an
appreciative note next morning to "dear David" from
"JT". The dress suit passed into the common currency
and was soon used by other cartoonists.'

Honourable J. H. Thomas, P. C., M. P.

# Second series

## Stanley Baldwin, Earl Baldwin of Bewdley (1867-1947)

● First published *New Statesman*, 4 November 1933 ● Lent by the British Museum

Conservative MP for Bewdley (1906-37); Chancellor of
the Exchequer (1922-23), Prime Minister (1923-24,
1924-29, 1935-37); Peer 1937

Baldwin was a conciliatory Tory whose moderation
helped weather the General Strike and Abdication
crisis. Out of his depth in foreign affairs, he did little
about the rise of Hitler.

Low: 'The one I like best is the Stanley Baldwin.
One night I shall burgle the British Museum, which
has the original, and steal it back.'

Mister Baldwin

LOW

# James Maxton (1885-1946)

● First published *New Statesman*, 2 December 1933
● Lent by Mr Alan Young

Independent Labour MP for Glasgow
Bridgeton (1922-46).
Maxton was a member of the left-wing Clydesiders
group, constant critics of the moderate policies
of the Labour Leader Ramsay McDonald.
According to Low, 'Most cartoonists have regarded
Maxton's policies as sinister, and they have therefore
given him a nasty look. In reality there is nothing
sinister about Maxton himself, excepting his black
forelock. When his face is not set "professionally",
so to speak, his eyes and mouth give him away as
being a kindly soul, and in private he enjoys a
remarkable popularity.'

95

# Sir John Simon, First Viscount Simon (1873-1954)

● First published *New Statesman*, 16 December 1933 ● Lent by the National Portrait Gallery

Liberal MP (1906-18, 1922-31); Liberal National MP
(1931-40); Solicitor-General (1910-13), Attorney-
General (1913-15), Home Secretary (1915-16),
Foreign Secretary (1931-35), Home Secretary
(1935-37), Chancellor of the Exchequer (1937-40),
Lord Chancellor (1940-45).
Low: 'Sir John Simon is a well-formed man,
but I sometimes draw him with a sinuous body
because that conveys more or less his disposition
to subtle compromise.'

# Ernest Bevin (1881-1951)

● First published *New Statesman*, 30 December 1933 ● Lent by the National Portrait Gallery

General Secretary of the Transport and General
Workers' Union (1921-41); Labour MP for
Wandsworth (1940-51); Minister of Labour (1940-45)
and a significant member of Churchill's War Cabinet;
Foreign Secretary (1945-50).
Low: 'The frequent use of "I" and "me" was
characteristic of Ernie's conversation. Such a vital and
forceful man just naturally came to identify the whole
Labour movement with himself.'

Ernest Bevin

## Sir George Ambrose Lloyd, First Baron Dolobran (1879-1941)

● First published *Ye Madde Designer*, Studio, 1935 ● Lent by The Political Cartoon Society

Governor of Bombay (1918-23), High Commissioner in Egypt (1923-29), Colonial Secretary (1940-41). Lloyd was a Tory die-hard, who when MacDonald's National Government resolved to give Dominion status to India, believed, along with Winston Churchill, that India was not ready for self-government. Lloyd saw such developments as the beginning of the end for British rule in India. He helped to form the 'India Defence Committee'; its objective was to oppose the government's proposals for Indian self-rule.

## William Wedgwood Benn, First Lord Stansgate (1877-1960)

● Lent by The Political Cartoon Society

Resigned as a Liberal MP to join the Labour Party; Labour MP for North Aberdeen (1927-31), Gorton (1937-40); Secretary of State for India (1929 31), Secretary of State for Air (1945-46); Peer 1940. The Peerage Act (1963) allowed his son, Anthony (Tony) Wedgwood Benn, to surrender his peerage to stand for election to the House of Commons.

111

# Harold Laski (1893-1950)

● First published *New Statesman*
● Lent by Low Family

Professor of Political Science at the London School of Economics. Laski was a committed socialist and in 1936 helped to form the Left Book Club with Victor Gollancz and Labour MP John Strachey to spread socialist ideas and resist the rise of fascism in Britain. Laski became chairman of the Labour Party in 1945. Low: 'Harold Laski's platform manner and utterance – feet wide apart, unexpectedly strong nasal voice – were easy to parody and there were very few of the bright boys who is not include them in his imitations.'

Harold Laski

## Anthony Eden, Earl of Avon (1897-1977)

- First published *The Prime Ministers*, George Malcolm Thompson, 1980
- Lent by Mr Reg Bass

Conservative MP for Warwick and Leamington (1923-59); Parliamentary Private Secretary to Austen Chamberlain (1926-29), Under Secretary for Foreign Affairs (1931-34), Foreign Secretary (1935-38, 1940-45, 1951-55), Prime Minister (1955-57); Peer 1961.

## Herbert, Baron Morrison (1888-1965)

- First published *Low's Company*, Methuen, 1952
- Lent by National Portrait Gallery

Labour MP for South Hackney (1923-59); Minister for Transport (1931), Leader of the London County Council (1934-40), Home Secretary (1940-45), Deputy Prime Minister and Leader of the House of Commons (1945-51), Foreign Secretary (1951); Life Peer 1959. Low first drew Morrison as the Mayor of Hackney. Thirty years later, Low wrote, 'How carefully since then we had both cultivated his hair into the celebrated Morrison quiff... He loved to see himself drawn, although I fear his judgement was affected too much by the degree of sympathy displayed in the representation.'

## Dr Edith Summerskill (1901-80)

- First published *Low's Company*, Methuen, 1952
- Lent by The Political Cartoon Society

Labour MP for Fulham West (1938-55),
Warrington (1955-61); Minister of National
Insurance (1950-51), Chair of the Labour
Party (1954-55); Life Peeress 1961.

## Richard Austen ('Rab') Butler (1902-82)

- First published *Low's Company*, Methuen, 1952
- Lent by The Political Cartoon Society

Conservative MP for Saffron Walden
(1929-65); Minister of Education (1941-45),
Chancellor of the Exchequer (1951-55),
Leader of the House of Commons (1955-57),
Home Secretary (1957-63), Foreign Secretary
(1963-64); Life Peer 1965.

# Low's influence on contemporary cartoonists

## Dave Brown, 'Empty Shoes'

● First published *New Statesman*, 21 March 1997 ● Lent by Mr Dave Brown

In March 1997, Prime Minister John Major knew his chances of winning the coming election were slim. The Conservative Party, in power for 18 years, was divided over Europe and troubled by scandal. It trailed the Labour Party consistently by approximately 20 points in the opinion polls. There were rumours at Westminster that certain Tory MPs were already posi-tioning for the inevitable leadership contest after the General Election, which was probably to be held in May. Ironically, Brown did not include William Hague, the victor, as a potential leadership contender. This cartoon alludes to Low's 'Empty Shoes' (below right), drawn in March 1953 after the death of Stalin; Malenkov and Beria wait outside the dead dictator's door.

## Steve Bell, 'Very Well, Alone'

● First published *The Guardian*, 22 March 1996
● Lent by Mr Steve Bell

On 20 March 1996, the Conservative government admitted that the brain disease, new variant CJD, was probably linked to BSE. It seemed that victims had caught the disease by eating meat from BSE-infected cattle. The European Union reacted by banning all exports of British beef to the continent. This cartoon is an allusion to Low's 'Very Well, Alone' (see cartoon number 44), when Britain stood alone against Nazi Germany after the fall of France in June 1940.

'VERY WELL, ALONE'

## Mac, 'They're Off!'

● First published *Daily Mail* 10 April 1979
● Lent by Mr Stan MacMurtry

On 28 March 1979, Prime Minister James Callaghan was defeated in a vote of confidence in the House of Commons by just one vote. Labour's minority Government was at an end. Parliament was dissolved on 7 April and a General Election called for 3 May. The memories of the 'Winter of Discontent' were a severe handicap for the Labour Party as, for many, it showed the unacceptable face of British Trade Unionism. The Conservatives, led by Margaret Thatcher, won a comfortable majority. Mac's image refers to Low's many versions of the TUC Carthorse (see, for example, number 80).

## Nick Garland, 'Rendezvous'

● First published *The Daily Telegraph* 22 March 1983
● Lent by Mr Nick Garland

On 26 March 1981, the Social Democratic Party was launched; it was mainly made up of Labour MPs who felt the Labour Party had swung too far to the Left. One of the SDP founders, Shirley Williams, won a by-election in a Conservative seat. Relief came for Labour leader Michael Foot in a by-election at Darlington in March 1983, where Labour candidate Ossie O'Brien defied expectations of a SDP win by holding the seat. This shored up Foot's leadership, but encouraged PM Margaret Thatcher to call an immediate election as his Labour Party was widely seen as unelectable. The Tories won a landslide and O'Brien lost the seat he had held for just six weeks. Low's original (inset) shows Hitler and Stalin greeting each other over the corpse of a Polish soldier.

## Martin Rowson, 'All behind you, Tony'

● First published *The Guardian*, 5 May 1997
● Lent by Mr Martin Rowson

On 2 May 1997, the Labour Party, under the leadership of Tony Blair, won a landslide General Election victory and returned to office for the first time since 1979. Rowson's image refers to Low's 'All Behind You, Winston' of May 1940 (cartoon number 42).

## Peter Brookes, 'Before/After'

- First published *The Times*, 9 October 2001
- Lent by Peter Brookes

President George W Bush ordered American air strikes on Afghanistan after Taliban leaders repeatedly refused to hand over Osama bin Laden, the prime suspect in the 11 September terrorist attacks on New York and Washington. On 7 October, the air campaign against the Taliban began with the heavy bombing of Afghanistan's capital, Kabul. Brookes makes the point that Kabul was already in ruins from years of civil war; a result of the power vacuum left by the Soviet Army's withdrawal in February 1989. The cartoon is not strictly an allusion to Low's 'Barbarism/Civilisation' (number 25) but one can clearly see the influence it had on Brookes.

BEFORE      AFTER

---

# Acknowledgements

This exhibition is held in Westminster Hall by kind permission of the Speaker, the Lord Chancellor and the Lord Great Chamberlain. *BBC History Magazine* and the Political Cartoon Society also wish to acknowledge the kind support of the House of Commons Advisory Committee on Works of Art, chaired by Tony Banks MP, and the House of Lords Advisory Panel on Works of Art, chaired by Baroness Hilton of Eggardon.

*BBC History Magazine* and the Political Cartoon Society wish to acknowledge the kind support of Atlantic Syndication and the Low Estate for granting copyright to the exhibition. The sponsors and organisers would like to thank those who have lent artworks for this exhibition.

**Curator** Timothy Benson
**Text** Alan Mumford (introduction), Timothy Benson (captions)
**Editor** Sarah Farley
**Designers** Andrew Ellis, Bettina Bard
**Picture Editors** Christine Hinze, Caroline Wood

**Picture acknowledgements**
© Atlantic Syndication: all cartoons and caricatures by Low and cartoon by Mac page 116 below
© Steve Bell 1996: page 116 above
© Peter Brookes/The Times, London: page 118
© Dave Brown 1997: page 115 left
Centre for the Study of Cartoons and Caricature, University of Kent, Canterbury: pages 23, 30, 39, 43, 44, 46, 51, 53, 54, 55, 63, 64, 65, 66, 70, 71, 73, 77, 78, 79, 92, 116 below, 117 below

Corbis: page 14 left (© Underwood & Underwood), page 14 right (© Bettmann)
Hulton|Archive: pages 12, 13, 15
National Portrait Gallery, London: page 110
© Eamonn McCabe: page 16 left
Press Association: page 9
© Martin Rowson 1997: page 117 below
© David Sillitoe/The Guardian: pages 16 right, 17 left
© Ralph Steadman; page 17 right
© Telegraph Group Limited 1983: page 117 above left